# Island Boy

## from the little village to the big city

By

Dhyan Lal

authorHOUSE®

*AuthorHouse™*
*1663 Liberty Drive*
*Bloomington, IN 47403*
*www.authorhouse.com*
*Phone: 833-262-8899*

*Published by AuthorHouse 07/08/2022*

*ISBN: 978-1-4208-4052-0 (sc)*
*ISBN: 978-1-4520-2970-2 (e)*

*Library of Congress Control Number: 2005903300*

*Print information available on the last page.*

# Dedication

This book is dedicated to: Leonard Howard De
Caux, who brought me to America from the Fiji Islands
and raised me as his own son;
my father, Uttam Lal, who made the decision to send
me with Len to seek education and a better life when I
was only thirteen years old; and
my brother Gautam, who was the "rock" of the
family; he looked after his younger siblings and gave us
the courage to pursue our dreams.

# Acknowledgments

This book could not have been written without the encouragement and support of my wife, Shirley; sons, Dhyan and Amrit; and daughter Roshni.

My special thanks to Garcie, who has been a true friend from the first day that I met him. Also, I owe my gratitude to all those individuals who helped me climb the ladder of success and realize the American Dream. Finally, a special thanks to Lesley Bolton for taking the time to edit.

# Table of Contents

# Prologue

I lay in the darkness staring at the white ceiling wondering if the life I was living was real or if I had just fallen asleep and commenced to dream. There was an eerie silence all around me. The bed was soft with blue blankets draped over the white sheets. There was a desk with a chair on one side of the room and a chest of drawers on the other side. I had my hands behind my head and was gazing at the popcorn ceiling. There was a slight chill in the air, but I did not bother getting under the blankets.

If this was a dream, then why did the images of the airport, people crying, and the vivid scene of me climbing into a huge airplane seem so real? What were these strange feelings and thoughts occupying my mind? I knew that at any minute either my mother or auntie would come bursting through the door yelling, "Wake up; it's time for school." But I did not have a separate room or a bed. The four brothers slept on the floor inside the mosquito net in the front room. Moreover, this was a soft bed in a bedroom, and there was no mosquito net. Was I dreaming?

Ever since I first met Len on that sunny, balmy day in Suva, when two of my friends and I ditched school to go see the tourist ship that was anchored in the harbor, I often dreamt about how it would be to live in America. I would close my eyes and imagine that I was sitting in the living room of a big house with four or five rooms, lots of furniture, electricity, a telephone, and other modern conveniences. People always spoke about this place called America, where money practically grew on trees; everyone lived in large homes and drove big cars. However, somehow my current dream appeared to be more genuine than all of my previous ones.

I must have fallen asleep because when I opened my eyes, I was not certain if this scenario was a dream or if I was merely waking up from a deep sleep. One thing was certain; I was still lying on the bed in an empty, strange room. This dream was beginning to scare me. I jumped out of the bed and ran through the hallway into the family room where I found Sylvia, Len's niece, and two of her daughters watching television. No, this was not a dream; I was at the house in Glendale, in America, far away from my home in Fiji.

Once the realization that I was not dreaming came to light and what appeared to be a dream was in essence my reality, strange thoughts began to invade my mind. Was I ever going to see my family again? What if these people in whose care I have been placed didn't like me? Would they throw me out into the strange world? As it was, I could hardly understand anything they were saying. What would I do all by myself, and where would I go? I wanted to run out of that room and keep on running until I could smell the fresh ocean air and see the familiar coconut trees swaying in the wind with clear blue waters hugging the white sandy beaches.

# Chapter One: Growing Up in Paradise

I was born in 1948 in the small town of Samabula, which is one mile from the capital city of Suva, in the Fiji Islands. Samabula was a small community with single-family homes, small shops, and neighborhood schools. The main road that passed through the middle of the town was narrow but tar sealed. Most of the other roads were either dirt or gravel. There was a large playground, Combine Ground, where all the athletic activities were held. This was where I spent a majority of my spare time playing soccer. Every afternoon, the ground was filled with soccer, rugby, and field hockey players practicing in different sections of the ground. Next to the ground was a field with an abundance of guava, mango, and papaya trees. Usually after playing at the ground, we headed for the field for ripe mangoes or guavas.

Samabula was a unique community because people of different ethnicities lived next to each other. We had Chinese, Fijians, Indians, Samoans, Tongans, and people from other Pacific Islands residing there. Unlike Samabula, a majority of the communities in the Islands was made up of one dominant race with a few families of other races interspersed throughout. Native Fijians and Indians made up the majority of the population. Fijians mostly lived in villages, as they had done for hundreds of years. The Indians, who were brought to Fiji by the British to work on the sugar cane plantations in the latter part of the 1800s, were interspersed throughout the Islands. A majority of the Indians lived in predominantly Indian communities with few Fijians and other Pacific Islanders as neighbors.

The British or any other whites did not live in any of the integrated areas. They lived in the exclusive "white" areas throughout the Islands. In the Suva area, they lived in Tamavua or Suva Point. Both of these areas were exclusive with large homes, manicured lawns, and domestic servants to cater to all their needs. Tamavua had a breathtaking view of the Suva Harbor and the countryside, and Suva Point was a community on the beach. Fiji was under the British rule until 1974 with a governor appointed by the British government. The heads of all the major departments of the government were white.

As children, we did not know too much about the political aspects of life. We enjoyed our families and the daily activities in and out of school. There were no ethnic or racial problems. We all knew about each other's cultures and enjoyed the festivities whenever one of the groups celebrated an event. Schools were configured along racial and ethnic lines—Indian, Fijian, and Moslem—but students were not prohibited from attending the school of their choice. Private and parochial schools were usually integrated. Nonetheless, the white children usually attended the British or international schools. The fees for these schools were high, precluding most of the locals from attending.

My grandparents from both sides had been brought from India as indentured servants. They arrived in the Islands at a very young age. I only remember my maternal grandfather. He was very old, about ninety, tall, slightly stooped over, and walked with a cane. When he came to visit us, he would tell us stories about how the British would make them work long hours on hot days without giving them breaks. Once, he told us a story about how a white man attempted to hit him with whip, but he grabbed the whip and gave the man a good hiding. They were servants, not slaves, and were not supposed to be whipped or brutalized in any manner. Indentured servants were free to go back to India after five years of service or stay in Fiji. A majority of the Indian people chose to stay in Fiji and carved a new life for themselves.

Both of my parents were born and raised in Fiji and grew up in large families. My father, Uttam Lal, was born in Samabula, and my mother, Phul Kuar, was born in a small village next to the Rewa River, the largest river in Fiji. She was born on a farm that was adjacent to the river. Neither one of my parents received any formal education. My father learned to be a mechanic, and later, during World War II, he became a driver for the Public Works Department of the Fiji government. His friendly personality and ability to get along with others made him popular with the Americans who were stationed in Fiji during World War II.

Fiji was deemed a strategic location in the South Pacific. The Japanese would have to navigate through Fiji waters to reach Australia, New Zealand, and other South Pacific Islands. My father was assigned to drive the American and British dignitaries. Because of his association with them, he was permitted to take home food items and goods that were not available to the rest of the people. The war had impeded shipments of goods from other countries that created a shortage for the islanders. My father shared the food and other items with the people of Samabula. Because of his generosity, everyone called him *bhai*, brother. To this day, we still refer to him as bhai. None of his children or nieces and nephews called him anything else.

My immediate family consisted of five brothers and three sisters. Gautam was the eldest in the family followed by sister Shri Mati, brother Gyan, me, sister Son Mati, brothers Amrit and Ashok, and the youngest sister, Angela. Since he was the older brother, Gautam had the responsibility of looking after all of us. He was an excellent student and athlete. He played soccer, rugby, and field hockey in school. Unfortunately, Gautam had to leave school in form five, equivalent to the junior year of high school in the United States, to help the family.

Attending high school was extremely expensive. Few people could afford to send their children beyond the eighth grade. If I had not migrated to the United States, I probably would have followed the same route as Gautam.

Shri Mati and Son Mati both went to an all-girls school and did not attend beyond the eighth grade either. Most girls in the islands either did not go to school or left school early to help their mothers with domestic chores.

As for Gyan, he hated school, and all he wanted to do was work on cars. He left school in the seventh grade to work as an auto mechanic for a relative. Gyan was quite talented when it came to fixing cars and other motorized equipment. He could barely read or write, but his talents made him invaluable to the people in the neighborhood. Today he is an aircraft mechanic.

My brother John was probably one of the smartest children in the family. When he was four years old, he could read, write, and speak clearly. Unfortunately he was given an overdose of medicine during the typhoid fever scare of 1954 that left him paralyzed and brain damaged. For the rest of his life he functioned like a six-month-old baby. My mother and sisters took care of John until he died at the age of twenty.

Ashok and Angela were very young when I left home. I became better acquainted with them during my visit in 1963. Angela was hit by a car when she was five years old and passed away in 1964. She was beautiful and bright. Angela did not want to leave my sight and made me promise that I would bring her over to America so she could be with me and receive a good education. Unfortunately, she did not live long enough to enjoy life in Fiji or anywhere else.

The island culture was such that families lived with each other and/ or very close together, and the neighbors were considered part of your family, related or not. This was a true village concept of living and raising families since everyone looked out for each other. For us, the children, this was a double-edged sword because if one of us was caught misbehaving, whoever caught us immediately punished us, and then we were punished again by our parents.

The home in which I grew up was a typical home in town, built of wood and tin with a corrugated tin roof. The house had two rooms: one was a tiny bedroom for the parents, and the other room was used as the living room, dining room, and a place for the children to sleep. We slept on the floor on mats called *chatai*. The kitchen was a small shack made of tin. It was detached from the house and located in the back. We had no electricity, indoor plumbing, or refrigeration. All variety of foods was bought every day from the local market or picked from our garden. The food was cooked outside on the open fire and sometimes on a kerosene burning apparatus known as a Primus.

Our mode of transportation consisted of either walking or traveling on buses. Since cars were a luxury that few people could afford, walking to destinations up to five miles was not uncommon. The buses were made of wood, had diesel engines, and had tarpaulin windows that were tied and hooked to the wooden frame. When it rained, the tarpaulin prevented some water from coming into the bus, but people who sat next to the windows were guaranteed to get soaked. These buses spewed black smoke as they ventured along the winding gravel roads. Riding on the buses was an adventure because within a ten-mile stretch, they went through areas that were overrun with thick vegetation, allowing barely enough room for the bus to pass.

Growing up in Fiji was an experience that in retrospect was both challenging and heavenly. My memory of the first five years of my life is a little hazy, but I do remember going to a Moslem school when I was five years old. This school was only two hundred yards from our house. One or two of the children living next to us attended this school so my parents decided to send me with my friends. The students all wore uniforms; girls wore green dresses, and the boys wore green shirts and khaki pants. Although the school followed a regular curriculum, at least one hour a day was spent studying the Islamic religion.

The teachers at Samabula Moslem School were strict to the point of being abusive. Islamic religion dictated the codes of conduct for students and teachers alike. Students were not permitted to question the teachers. I thoroughly despised the first-grade teacher, who seemed to enjoy beating the students, especially me because I always asked for a reason for teaching us a specific element. One day, I asked him a question as to why his religion was different from mine and whose god was more powerful. He did not answer me, so I asked again. He became angry, walked over, and began hitting me on the head with the ruler. He was angry because I was asking for an answer that probably involved some discussions that in his mind were too sophisticated for a five-year-old. Perhaps he figured that I was being insolent and degrading his religion.

I went home crying with bumps on my head. My uncle, Chandar Lal, who lived with us and treated us as if we were his own children, saw me crying, looked at the bumps and bruises, and became very angry. He asked me what happened, and I told him that the teacher hit me. He went to the school the next day to confront the teacher, who refused to meet him because he knew that my uncle was going to give him a good thrashing. My uncle went to see the headmaster to discuss the incident. The headmaster told him that I was being disrespectful to the teacher and creating a problem in the class. After giving the headmaster a piece of his mind, my uncle checked me out of the school.

Chandar Lal, known as *kaka*, was my father's younger brother. Their parents had passed away when kaka was young. They had two older sisters who were already married, had moved in with their husbands' families, and were raising their own children. As is customary in the Islands, families usually lived together; it was only natural that my uncle lived with us. Both my father and uncle worked for the Public Works Department of the government as light truck drivers.

Kaka was strict with us, but also very caring when it came to our well-being. He made sure that we went to school every day, had all the school supplies, and behaved ourselves at all times. He was more like an older brother who assumed the role of a father whenever necessary. He was about five feet nine inches tall with black hair, very thin, and always had a smile on his face. Like bhai, kaka was an excellent mechanic. On weekends, both brothers spent their time fixing old cars for friends or relatives.

After taking me out of the Moslem school, kaka enrolled me into the public school, known as Samabula Government School, an all-boys school. Although it was known as a government school, we had to pay fees to attend. There was no such thing as free education; all schools charged fees. Most of the neighborhood Indian boys attended Samabula Government School. Those families who had money sent their children to parochial schools. Some of my cousins and friends attended Saint Columbus School. The fees for Saint Columbus were higher, and all the subjects were taught in English. Students attending there did not learn to read or write Fijian or Hindi.

Samabula Government School's ethnic population was 99 percent Indian and the other 1 percent Fijian. All faculty members were of Indian descent. Everyone paid school fees of approximately $15 a quarter for four quarters. The family income ranged from $10 to $20 a week. My father's wages were $12 a week. Not only did we have to pay school fees, but we also had to purchase all our supplies, including textbooks. The uniform of the school was a white shirt and khaki shorts.

The school was comprised of several stand-alone wood and tin buildings. Each classroom accommodated approximately forty-five students. We sat on wooden chairs with tables for writing. At the primary level, a slate and pencil were used for writing. Once a lesson was completed, we erased the slate and worked on the new subject. Only homework was done on writing paper. For writing, we either used a pencil or pen and nib. The nib was dunked into a bottle filled with ink in order for us to write. The nib was usually empty after two or three lines, necessitating another dunk in the ink bottle.

I enjoyed attending my new school. On the first day, I met with most of the boys and immediately established friendships, some of which have remained until today. We all came from a similar working-class background. Our lives as well as our interests were simple. In the classroom, we were all very quiet and attended to our tasks. However, during the breaks, we played hard and loudly. Our games usually consisted of soccer, rugby, or hide and seek. On rainy days, we purposely played soccer so we would get wet and muddy, and hoped to be sent home by the teacher.

School was a place where we went to learn, but most of all, we went to play. Every day was filled with fun and excitement. I liked school and looked forward to going. Daily, I was up early, ate breakfast, and waited for my friends to whistle, giving me the signal that it was time to go. We walked about a mile to school. Those students who lived too far away usually traveled by bus.

When I wasn't playing soccer or in class, I was off with my friends fishing, swimming, or exploring some of the heavily forested areas. Life was filled with adventures, thrills, and challenging experiences. There was a core group of us who always hung around together in and out of school. We considered each other as brothers and never let anyone put us down or place us in dangerous situations. We cared for each other in every aspect. Sometimes our adventures almost got us into trouble. Like the time we followed an underground stream that meandered for approximately half a mile and suddenly became a waterfall. One of my friends who wasn't paying attention slipped, fell, and almost got carried away by the water. Luckily he grabbed a bamboo plant, or he would have fallen at least fifty feet.

My friend Ashraf (the gangster) was a very loyal and caring individual. He came from a large family of six brothers and five sisters. His father was a cook for one of the British families and was rarely home during the daylight hours. Ashraf was a rebel who did not take orders from anyone. He had his problems with authority and some of the "heavy-handed" adults, but he always looked out for his friends. He was genuine in his beliefs and had a good heart. Ashraf did not perform well academically, but outside of the classroom, he was a survivor and very smart about the ways of the world.

I always make a concerted effort to find Ashraf whenever I visit Fiji. When I went back to Fiji in 1966, I was told that Ashraf was in jail because he refused to obey a policeman and got into a fight. I wasn't surprised. He never backed down from anyone when he knew he was right. I remember when we were in class six; the teacher accused me of throwing a piece of paper on the floor. Ashraf immediately told him that it was not me. The teacher asked him to name the culprit, but Ashraf refused. He received a good hiding from the teacher for being disrespectful. I will never forget that scene when Ashraf almost hit the teacher but instead ran out of the classroom and never returned.

# Chapter Two: Samabula

Samabula was more like a big village than a town. No one could make a move without someone knowing about it. I remember once when some of my friends and I decided to ditch school and go swimming at the nearby beach. It was a typical South Seas Island day, with warm sunshine and cool trade winds blowing. The air had a sweet, fresh smell. It was a perfect day to be outside enjoying the tropical climate and not to be sitting in a classroom. We all met at a corner by Combine Ground and walked about a mile to a secluded swimming area. The water was warm with just a slight ripple. Hurriedly, we took off our clothes, placed them neatly on top of our books, and dove into the water.

An older brother of one of our friends had seen us leave and followed us to the beach. After we had taken our plunge and were fully enjoying ourselves for about an hour, one of the boys said he thought he saw a shadow move through the trees. Before any one of us could say anything, a figure appeared from the bushes and came toward us. "Get out of the water and get dressed," he yelled. "Now walk back to school." We were terrified about what was going to happen once we arrived at school.

Our captor proudly informed the teacher about our escapade. The teacher lined all six of us in front of the class, took out his ruler, and hit us six times on each palm, one strike for each one of us. Then he told us to tell our parents what had happened. Of course, we dared not hide anything from our parents. Even if we did not tell, they probably already knew before we arrived home from school.

When I came home, my father had already heard about my beach outing through the island grapevine. He simply looked at me and told me to stand in the corner with my face against the wall until he was ready to figure out my punishment. I stood against the wall for three hours. From my point of view, this was punishment enough, but bhai thought otherwise. He sternly stipulated that I could not play soccer or go to the movies for two weeks and had to be home immediately after school every day. This was a severe punishment for me since I loved playing soccer after school. Usually, I came home just before dark. Most of the time, I was able to argue my way out of any difficult situation; bhai called me the little lawyer. I was verbal with an excellent auditory memory. I always achieved a class rank of first or second out of thirty-five to forty students.

On weekends, we usually went to visit one of our relatives, or they came to visit us. Though none of the relatives lived far away, it seemed as if we were traveling a long distance whenever we went somewhere. I looked forward to visiting my cousins, especially those who lived close to a river or the beach. We went fishing, played various games, or jumped into the river for a refreshing swim. There is something soothing about palm trees swaying, the leaves hissing in the gentle breeze, and gazing at the colorful water. When I am in the water, looking at the sky and the trees, all the problems of the world seem unimportant and inconsequential. Even today, when I go back to the Islands, I sit on the beach or at the edge of the river and look at the peaceful surroundings. The serenity of the setting with the mild breeze gives me inner peace.

By the time I was in the third grade, I undertook the risk of challenging the teachers on some of what they were expounding. For the insolence, I usually ended up getting into trouble. My punishment often consisted of sweeping and mopping the classroom and scrubbing the desks.

I remember vividly once not standing for the national anthem, "God Save the Queen," at an assembly. The headmaster asked, "Why didn't you stand up for the flag salute and national anthem?"

"She is not my queen, so I did not feel like standing," I replied.

"You insolent delinquent," he yelled and smacked me right across the face. Then he grabbed a guava stick and gave me a thrashing.

I continued my protest and said, "She is the queen of the British who look down upon us; why should we stand for their flag or country's song?" I have always believed in doing the right thing, not just doing things to cater to someone else. Of course, my actions have sometimes led to dire consequences.

# Chapter Three: Searching for Religion

My parents were very religious. They practiced Hinduism. They were always going to different temples and praying to the countless Hindu gods. I accompanied them on some of these religious outings. In fact, I attended churches of every denomination with my Christian friends, Mosques with my Moslem friends, the Sikh Temple, and other places of worship. My curiosity led me to explore all these religions. One thing about the British was that they gave the people the freedom to practice the religion of their choice. I discovered that all the religions preached the same message of a higher being guiding our lives and if we were not good, the higher being would punish us. No matter what faith I was exploring, I always had questions for the priest, pundit, or whoever was the headman. I wanted to know whom they were chosen by to be the representatives of their Supreme Being, and how they communicated with their gods.

Of course, nobody was ever able to give me a straight answer. They told me god was everywhere, he was in heaven looking down at us, or he would come to me if my belief was strong. All of these answers had one thing in common: If individuals did not believe, they would go to a place where they would burn eternally. However, those who believed in god inherited a place called "heaven" that was filled with serenity and peace.

To me, the description of heaven sounded like Fiji. Every religion had the concept of heaven and hell.

I continued attending the various houses of worship looking for a meaning behind all the mumbo jumbo. My inquiries led to a conclusion that all the religions were about keeping people together and providing them a place for social gatherings where rituals were followed and certain codes of conduct were perpetuated. I rather enjoyed going to the churches, Hindu temples, and Islamic mosques. I specifically liked watching people's behavior in their respective religious settings. Some people who were downright nasty to everyone and did not show compassion for their fellow humans behaved as if they were the saviors of the human race when they attended their houses of worship.

Through my search for the meaning of life and purpose of religion, I have found that one does not need to go to a building to pray to a deity or gather in mass with others to express one's beliefs. The concept of "God" is steeped in how one lives his or her life. I believe in helping people, being honest, and caring for those who are unable to care for themselves. Many who purport to be religious are actually hypocrites who lack the decency to be kind to others. I believe in my family and myself. Strength comes from believing in oneself, and that strength precludes the necessity to believe in some external force for guidance.

# Chapter Four:  Family Life

Attending school and family gatherings was the highlight of my early years. Human beings need the company and comfort of each other. All the materialistic possessions can be taken away, but the feeling of love and compassion is irreplaceable. Life without friends and family is an empty existence. I truly feel that getting together with the family and friends to share beautiful moments and explore the mysteries of life creates positive energy. People who do not have love in their lives are lonely, bitter, and constantly in search of such comforts through other means.

Bhai and kaka always planned weekend outings at the beach or a river where we could fish. Kaka taught us how to swim when we were very young. His method of teaching my cousins, brothers, and me to swim was unique. He walked with us into the water until he was waist high, picked us up, counted to three, and threw us in the water. As we screamed and panicked, he simply told us how to move our arms and legs. It took us very little time to realize that we had to follow his instructions if we wanted to stay alive. Of course, the water was warm and calm and not deep enough to cause any one of us to drown. He wanted us to be independent and resourceful.

We never had to fear the water being cold or a wave knocking us around. A reef surrounds Fiji, so there are no waves on the beaches. Since Fiji is a tropical island lying just below the equator, there are only two seasons: summer and winter. Fiji's summer months are from October to March when the weather is hot, humid, and wet. The winter months are from April to September when it is mostly cool, 70 to 80 degrees, and dry with little or no humidity. The water temperature is always between 70 and 80 degrees. There are no known dangerous animals or sea creatures. I have heard about sea snakes, but we never encountered any.

After swimming, we were usually treated to a scrumptious island lunch consisting of a variety of food. We had traditional Fijian food such as Taro and Cassava, and Indian curries of various kinds, and a medley of fruits. Of course, every meal consisted of some kind of seafood. To this day, I can taste the hot spicy crab curry with rice or fresh fish cooked over the open fire. It was our job to go and find pieces of wood and husks of dried coconuts for the fire. We took a great delight in running along the beach and competing to see who could bring back the most husks and wood.

Sweet, delicious watermelon was always an ecstasy after a spicy meal. The children enjoyed spitting the seeds all over the place as they ran around with their faces pink from the watermelon. After lunch, it was time to take a nap, go back into the water, or attempt to catch the little crabs that came out of the sand. The adults sat under the swaying palm or mango trees and played cards. During the game, stories about people in the community or some of the gossip that was making its rounds through the island grapevine were shared.

When I was about eight years old, I began to work part-time at a little store across the street from our house helping the owner with small chores. A Chinese man fondly known as "Lolly," an English word for candy, owned the store. He received his nickname because whenever people shopped there, he would call to the young children and ask, "Do you want a lolly?" He had migrated from Hong Kong, leaving behind his wife and two children. Lolly regularly spoke about bringing his wife and children to Fiji after he had saved enough money.

Lolly had taken a liking to me and paid me one shilling for about two hours of work each day. My work consisted of filling the empty bottles with kerosene, bagging and weighing certain grocery items, and sweeping the store. If he needed extra work done, he would give me an additional sixpence or some candy. On weekends, my brother Gyan, who is two years older than me, and I washed cars and cleaned the dirt from potatoes and onions imported from Australia and New Zealand for a big grocery store. We used the money to go to the movies and for other entertainment.

My father struggled to pay the school fees for all of us. Bhai was a proud man who never wanted a hand or a handout. He used to say, "If your kaka and I cannot provide for you, then the oldest one of you will have to work to help the family." Several of my friends dropped out of school by the time they were in the sixth grade because their parents could not pay the school fees. I was always conscious of the fee problem, but never wanted to burden my parents by nagging them when it came time to pay. On one such occasion, the teacher told two of my friends and me not to come to school if we did not have our fees. Instead of telling our parents about our plight, we decided that we would go fishing and try to sell the fish to make some money.

The next morning, one of the boys suggested that instead of fishing, we should go to the harbor to see if we could make money from the tourists by carrying their bags or by diving for coins. He said, "I was in town one day with my mother, and there was a big ship at the harbor. The white people on the ship were throwing money, and kids like us were diving to retrieve the coins as they hit the water. Some of the boys made one or two pounds by jumping and catching the money. A big American ship is in the harbor right now, and tourists are all over town shopping for souvenirs." I had only seen a passenger ship from far away, and the prospect of seeing a huge ship up close and making money by helping tourists carry their purchases back to the ship was enticing.

We hopped on the bus and headed for town. Suva was a big city to us. After all, we were ten years old, so just about everything looked big. As the bus made its way down the road and neared the bus stand, I turned around and caught a glimpse of this huge ship with the name *ORIANA* printed on the backside. The gigantic chimney that looked like a tall ten-story building was bellowing black smoke. I was in awe. How could something so big and heavy float on the water? A small rock sinks as soon as it is thrown in the water, yet this monstrous thing was going across the ocean with such ease. The ship was so gigantic that the people standing on the top of it looked like ants.

The closer we got to the ship, the more perplexed I became about its ability to float. I had made small wooden boats and floated them down a stream, but something as big as the *ORIANA* made out of steel completely baffled me. I stood there looking up, straining my neck and admiring the ship for quite a while. Then I prepared myself to dive for the coins being tossed by the tourists. One of the boys said, "Hey, let's go by the market and see if we can talk to some tourists and carry the souvenirs they buy. They will pay us."

"No, let's stay here and see if we can catch some of the money being thrown from the ship," I answered. My buddies were afraid to jump into the water. After a brief discussion, I gave into their demand.

A few minutes later, we walked back to the marketplace and approached the tourists who were loaded down with souvenirs. In our limited and broken English, we asked if we could help them carry their bags back to the ship. Usually, when we carried people's belongings, they gave us 50 cents or a dollar. Of course, this was big money for us. It was still early and not too many tourists had come off the ship to start their shopping spree. We stood around and waited. Some of the tourists we approached were nasty and told us to get away from them, but most of them were cordial and simply said, "No, thanks."

# Chapter Five: Meeting Len

The three of us stood there smiling at the tourists as they passed by. One of the tourists smiled back and nodded his head. He appeared to be in his fifties, about six feet tall, and 180 pounds with a slightly protruding stomach, and he wore a baseball cap. I said, "Hello. Can we show you around town?"

He stopped, looked at us, smiled, and said, "Okay." He asked us for our names and told us that his name was Len.

"Where are you from?" I asked.

"The United States," he responded with a smile that revealed the gold on his right canine teeth.

After giving him our names, which he pronounced with great difficulty, we attempted to carry on a conversation. When we did not understand what he said, we smiled, which was quite often. We proceeded to show Len around what we considered to be our fantastic city, Suva. At one point, Len stopped and asked, "Do you boys want something to eat or drink?"

I immediately said, "I would love some ice cream." The other two boys looked at Len and nodded their heads in agreement. Actually, we were in front of an ice-cream parlor, and the pictures on the wall influenced my quick response. Once we were in the parlor, Len asked us to order whatever we wanted. This was unusual. All our lives we only received what was given to us; we were not given a choice from an unlimited selection without any regard for cost.

All three of us ordered Tiptop Ice Cream with Jell-O. Tiptop was the local brand of ice cream. This was the first time that any one of us had sat and eaten in an ice-cream parlor like the white or rich people did. In fact, the only time we ate ice cream with Jell-O was during Christmas. My uncle would bring the ice-cream maker and mix ice, rock salt, milk, sugar, and all the other ingredients that were required to make ice cream. This was an all-day event, and everyone took turns turning the handle to grind and mix the ingredients. Since Christmastime was the hottest time of the year, anything cold was a big treat.

Len asked, "So, do you boys go to school?" The three of us glanced at each other, trying to give the right answer.

"Yes," I replied before one of my colleagues could respond. "We attend Samabula Government School."

"Is today a school holiday for you boys?"

"No, we decided to take a day off to see the big boat. We have never seen anything so big on the water in our life. We saw that you were alone and thought you could use our help in getting around the town." I was ashamed to let him know that we had ditched school and were hustling to make some money.

As we left the ice-cream parlor, I looked back and wondered about the next time that I would be able to sit in style and enjoy ice cream. Walking through Suva, we pointed out to Len some of the landmarks and areas of interest. We strolled through the narrow streets for at least four hours. It was approaching 2:00 PM; Len turned to me and asked, "Is there a place where I could take a nap?" We were close to the botanical gardens, a park-like setting with beautiful flowers, big shady trees, a pond with beautiful water lilies, and a fountain in the middle. This was one of the most beautiful gardens in Fiji. I suggested that we walk to the garden, and he could take a nap under a tree. Len smiled and nodded his head, saying, "Yeah, sounds like a good idea." The day was rather warm so lying under a Banyan tree whose branches stretched forever next to a fountain seemed like an ideal place to relax.

The garden was located between Albert Park, Fiji's premier soccer and rugby grounds at that time, and the governor's house. The governor's house had immaculately manicured grounds with two guards dressed in the traditional British uniforms standing at the front gate. Across the park was the Grand Pacific Hotel, the pride of the Pacific. The GPH, as it was called, was built during World War II and was the first hotel in Fiji. It had all the elegance of a grand European hotel.

Located at the back of the botanical garden was the Fiji Museum. I had only been to the museum once, during a first-grade field trip. At that age, I had little understanding of the museum and did not appreciate the historical significance of the items on display. As Len took his nap, the three of us decided to explore the park and the museum. I was fascinated by the artifacts that were on display and the accounts of how the natives arrived in the Islands. I knew we were called the "Cannibal Islands," but to actually see pictures of some of the ferocious warriors was a revelation that lent credence to what we were learning in school about our history.

We spent over an hour running through the museum. It was around 3:30 when we walked back to the place where Len was napping. He was awake and looking at the sky. He turned, smiled, and said, "So there you are. This is quite a big beautiful tree, and look at that clear blue sky." He said that he had a very relaxing nap and thanked us for bringing him to such a beautiful spot. Len looked at his watch and said that we had better head back because the ship was leaving at around 5:00 PM. It was about a half-hour walk back to the harbor.

I accompanied Len and my friends for approximately halfway, turned to him, and said, "One of the biggest soccer games is being played at Albert

22

Park at 5:00, and I really want to see it." I apologized for not walking all the way back with him.

He smiled at me and replied, "I don't mind walking back alone if you boys want to go to the game." My two friends said they did not care about the game and would walk back to the ship with him. Len gave me a hug and said goodbye. In saying goodbye, I felt an inexplicable feeling of sadness.

Walking back toward Albert Park, I stopped, looked back, and yelled, "Would you send us postcards from America?"

He replied, "Yeah!"

I ran back and gave him the address of the general post office in Samabula. When we parted, I found myself constantly turning around to wave and say goodbye. Little did I know that a tourist who I was sad to leave would someday become my surrogate father. That when I was thirteen years old, Len would come back to visit Fiji, spend three weeks with the family, and sponsor me to study in America—an event that would change not only my life, but also the lives of my entire family, including the extended family.

During the next several weeks, I constantly stopped by the post office to inquire if there was any mail for me. The answer given by the postman was always the same: "No, there is nothing here for you." It had been about six weeks since we first met Len, and we did not hear from him. I thought briefly that if he were going to write to us, he would have done so by now, but I did not give up hope and visited the post office at least twice a week. Perhaps his writing to us was delayed due to obligations he had to meet after being away for so long.

One day, I dropped by the post office with the usual question, and the postman said, "Yes, there is a letter for you from America." He continued, "Two other boys had letters too, but they picked up theirs yesterday." I was bewildered to find that my friends had not informed me about the letter from Len. In my eagerness to open the letter, I tore the envelope into several pieces. Concealed inside the written page were a postcard and a $5 bill.

Len expressed his gratitude to us for showing him the town and spending the day with him. He said, "I had a great time being escorted by three local boys and engaging in conversations with you, even if you didn't understand most of what I was saying." He asked me if I had received the money that he had given to my friends to give to me. He wrote, "I gave $5 each to the other boys and asked them to give you the other $5." Of course, my friends neglected to tell me about the money, which only meant that they kept the money and divided my portion between them.

When I saw my two friends the next day, I asked, "Where is the $5 the white man we met gave to you for me?"

They glanced at each other, shrugged their shoulders, looked back at me, and responded, "What money? We don't know what you are talking about." I knew that they were lying and had made a pact to stick to their story. I chose not to confront them any further. In my reply to Len, I told him about the behavior of my friends, their total denial of receiving any money from him. I also thanked him for the postcard and the money. Len wrote back within two weeks with a $10 bill and an American shirt for me. The other two boys never bothered to respond to the first letter. All they cared about was the money and figured that there was no sense in communicating with someone they would never see again.

My correspondence with Len continued for two years, 1959 to 1961. He sent money for me to buy gifts for my brothers and myself. Len also sent money to the family to insure that our school fees were paid, and we had the necessary books. In one of the letters, he stated, "I would like to visit Fiji again and meet your family. I feel that I know them already and want to see them." We wrote back letting Len know that everyone would be delighted to meet him and have him in our home. Of course, we did not know when he would be coming or for how long. We really did not have any place for him to sleep. Even so, the invitation was extended to Len to visit the family and stay with us.

In June of 1961, Len came to Fiji. My father, uncle, oldest brother, a friend of the family, and I went to pick up Len from the airport in Nadi, about 150 miles from Suva. This was my first visit to the airport, and I was eager to see an airplane land. When I first saw the huge ship float on the water, I was amazed, but seeing an airplane fly like a bird was beyond comprehension. Once the plane had landed and the door opened, we all strained our necks to find Len. It was not difficult to see Len getting off the plane, because not too many tourists visited Fiji. I had given everyone a description of Len, so locating him was not a chore. Gautam spotted him right away and waved with both hands. Len waved back with a pleasant smile on his face. He walked over, shook hands with everyone, and gave me a big hug. At first, I was shy, but I returned his hug and said, "Good to see you." We proceeded to the baggage claim area to retrieve Len's luggage.

Len was conversing with the adults, but he turned around and smiled at me every once in a while. Gautam asked, "So, how was your flight?"

"It was very comfortable. I stopped in Honolulu and visited with some friends for a few days, so the flight did not seem so long," Len replied. While we were waiting for the luggage, we could see people with inquisitive looks on their faces attempting to figure out what this white man was doing with the locals. Heads were still turning when we walked out of the airport. In the sixties, white people did not mix with the locals. So, to see a white person with an Indian or Fijian family was an enigma.

The ride from the airport to our home was long and dusty. Roads in Fiji were not paved. It took us over six hours through the windy, narrow, unpaved main highway to reach home. One good thing about this tedious journey was that the road ran along the coast, so we were treated to some of the most beautiful scenery in the world. Len admired the multicolored water and the white, sandy beaches. But he was too tired from the long plane ride to really enjoy anything.

It was a beautiful sunny day with a few white clouds moving across the blue sky. The ocean shimmering in the sunlight reflected the colors of the coral, giving the water blue, green, purple, pink, and turquoise hues. The coconut trees swaying over the water added to the beauty of the coastline. The coconut trees bending over the white sand along the blue water presented a picturesque view. About halfway home, we stopped at a store; my uncle bought a loaf of bread, sardines, an onion, and some lemonade for lunch. We found a beautiful spot along the beach to eat our "Fijian" picnic sandwiches.

As the car pulled close to our house, I could see my mother, brothers, sisters, and extended family members standing in the front waiting. Len saw this rather large group and commented, "Oh boy, you have the whole community out here." He was delighted to see all the people who had turned out to welcome him. After he managed to get his cramped legs out of the car, he stood up and greeted everyone with the familiar "How yea." From the moment he met my mother, whom we called "amma" (the Hindi word for mother), he too began addressing her as amma. And he addressed my father as "bhai" (the Hindi word for brother).

Since the letter of Len's impending visit was received, a new twin bed was bought and placed in the front room where all of us siblings slept on the floor. They also bought a tiny table with two chairs and placed it in the corner. When Len came in, my father and he sat at the table while the rest of us sat on the floor. My mother and some of the ladies immediately went to the kitchen, which was outside, and made tea. Tea and biscuits was an afternoon's delight that we always looked forward to.

Family members and visitors sat on the floor and stared at Len. A majority of the people did not speak English, so they did not understand most of the conversation that was taking place between bhai and Len. Whenever Len spoke to them, they smiled and nodded. Our living room was packed with people. More people kept on stopping by throughout the afternoon and evening. Bhai asked Len about America, where he lived, and about his own children. He expressed his delight in having Len visit and stay with us. Gautam also engaged in conversations with Len. This was a great opportunity for Gautam to practice his English.

It was close to dinnertime, and the crowd had somewhat thinned. We wondered what kind of food Len liked. My uncle who had worked with Americans and Europeans knew how to cook their food. He asked Len about dinner and what he preferred to eat. He replied, "Anything, except for the things that are too spicy." Kaka cooked chicken, potatoes, carrots, and greens for dinner. This special dinner was for Len and the adult males. The rest of us ate curry, rice, and roti, a thicker and moister version of totilla. Len was self-conscious about being the only one sitting at a table eating with a knife and fork while the rest of us sat on the floor eating with our hands. He told bhai, "You did not have to go through the trouble of making me a special meal."

Bhai replied, "You are the honored guest, and it is a pleasure to make a special meal for you. It is not every day that we have an American in our house."

Dinnertime was filled with idle chatter and curiosity about Len. More people were dropping by to say hello and shake Len's hand. As the evening wore on, Len began to yawn. Bhai asked, "Would you like to freshen up?" Len nodded his head. Gautam showed him the bathroom, which was located outside, not too far from the kitchen. While Len was getting ready, my mother fixed his bed. My aunt and mother had gone to town earlier in the day and bought new sheets, pillows, blankets, and a mosquito net. They wanted to make sure that Len was comfortable and not eaten by the mosquitoes at night.

It rained a lot on our side of the island, so we had a problem with mosquitoes. But there was no need to worry; we all slept inside mosquito nets. Len smiled when he saw the mosquito net over his bed. As soon as he lay down, we all threw our sheets over the chatai and got inside the big mosquito net. Everyone took a big delight in yelling, "Good night, Len."

Being good natured, Len responded to each one of us individually with a hardy, "Good night and see you in the morning."

Breakfast time was adventurous and a bit comical. Since the new twin bed was placed in the living room, one of the chickens decided to lay her eggs under the bed each morning. The chicken would run into the house around 7:00 AM, go under the bed, and lay her egg. Seeing how this chicken was our only source of fresh eggs, we could not serve Len his breakfast until the chicken had finished laying the egg.

The first morning, as Len was walking back from brushing his teeth, he saw the chicken dart out from under the bed cackling. He was not quite sure what was happening, but he did not see any of us terribly upset about the chicken being in the house. After witnessing the same scene the next day, Len looked at me and asked, "Why does the chicken like going under the bed?" I did not know what to say and looked in my brother's direction. Gautam enlightened Len about the saga of the chicken, and they both laughed.

Len visited with us for three weeks. Each day of the three weeks was an adventure for Len, my family, and me. Gautam took time off from work, and I stayed home from school to be with Len. For the first couple of days, all the adults and children stayed home. We went to lunch and dinner at the homes of various relatives and visited points of interest around town. After all, this was a historical event that no one wanted to miss.

During one of these outings, we were invited to a luncheon in the countryside on an island. Approximately eight of us went to the luncheon. The island was about ten miles from where we lived. To reach our destination, we had to travel by cars and then take a small boat along the river. When we reached the edge of the river, a small boat was waiting for us. We climbed into the boat one by one, assisted by the boatman. I was not paying attention and put one foot into the mud, causing concern and laughter.

After I rinsed my muddy legs, the boatman revved his Johnson 25 horsepower outboard engine and took off for about a twenty-minute ride. As the boat moved along the river, we were treated to beautiful, serene countryside. Along the river, we saw farms with cows and goats grazing, people fishing along the riverbanks, and women washing clothes. As the boat passed, the people waved, yelling, "Bula," the traditional Fijian greeting for hello. A slight wind was blowing, causing the coconut trees to sway. The river was calm, almost like glass. Our boat parted the water, causing ripples that flowed like musical notes toward the edge.

When we reached our destination, the boatman called out toward the house we were visiting. A man came out of the house waving his hand. He recognized my uncle and father, but he looked rather astonished. He welcomed us and invited us to some lemonade, cookies, and fried cassava and taro. We sat in the shade of a huge mango tree. Some ladies brought lemonade, fried taro, and cookies. The man, a relative, asked my father, "What brought you out here today?"

My father looked at him and replied, "The lunch invitation of course."

Our host shook his head, glanced in bhai's direction, and stated, "But the lunch invitation is next week."

Bhai was appalled and became very upset. He spoke to our host in Hindi so Len could not understand. Soon after we finished our drinks, bhai and kaka said it was time to go. We all looked at each other and headed toward the boat. The boatman realized what had happened and said, "We are going to a nice place along the river where there are many fruit and coconut trees, where we can have a nutritious lunch." He uttered, "The white man will really enjoy this place." Our hosts had not been prepared to serve us lunch and had no means of getting groceries since all stores in Fiji were closed on Sundays. Len did not know about the mix-up and thought that the destination was the actual place we were invited to for lunch.

The boat pulled along the river and came to a stop at a beautiful grassy area surrounded by coconut, papaya, mango, guava, and other fruit trees. We climbed out of the boat and sat on the riverbank in the soft grass. The boatman and some of the adults picked fruits while two teenagers from the nearby village climbed the tall coconut trees and broke the green coconuts for us to quench our thirst. The green coconuts have clear, sweet water inside them and soft meat, the taste of which is unparalleled. To say that I made a pig of myself would be an understatement.

Gautam and some of the young boys from the nearby village pulled some taro and cassava roots and threw them over the open fire. We ate the taro and cassava along with all the other tropical treats. Len thanked the boatman and the other people who helped us with our meal. He looked at my father and expressed his appreciation for such a fantastic meal in such beautiful surroundings. As the day wore on, we began to make our way back home. On the way back, everyone was quiet. They were either tired from the outing or too full to talk. Some of us, including Len, fell asleep in the car.

Within a few days, Len felt at home and established his daily routine. If we did not go anywhere special, we went into town and browsed. Len was amazed at the number of people my brother Gautam knew. We could not walk more than a few steps without someone coming up to him and striking up a conversation or someone yelling from across the street and waving. My brother would also encourage Len to stop in at the local pubs and grab a glass of beer every few hours. Those two really hit it off and became very close.

We would usually get home around the same time my father and uncle came home from work. Bhai and Len would sit out on the porch and talk about the day's events while drinking tea. People from the neighborhood would line up to see this white man staying with the locals. School children passing by would wave and stop just to look. Len would always wave back with a smile and say, "Hi. How are you?" After the tea, bhai would tell us to make a bowl of kava. This was a local drink that was made from the ground root of the pepper tree. It had a muddy appearance and little or no distinctive taste. Kava was a very popular drink in the Pacific Islands. Although kava was not intoxicating, it did leave one feeling numb and tingly if enough of it was consumed.

One peculiar thing that I never understood was that there were always a few people dressed in trench coats standing across the street or a few houses down watching our house. These individuals also followed us around in town. I figured that they were curious about the white man hanging out with us. It was not until Len had departed from Fiji that I learned that these men were from the CID, the Central Intelligence Division of Fiji Police.

Every evening we had the same scenario: the adult males sitting on the porch talking and drinking kava, the ladies cooking, and the children playing. One evening, the conversation was about education and the future of bright students in Fiji. My father told Len that those people who had money sent their children overseas for higher education. Fiji did not have a university, just a few technical schools.

Bhai informed Len that he could not afford to send his children overseas because of the family's financial situation. I heard my name mentioned, so I eavesdropped. I overheard bhai saying, "Dhyan is very good in school. He always comes first or second in his class, but high school is the limit for him unless he receives a scholarship from Australia, England, or New

Zealand." At that point, I was called away and was unable to hear the rest of the discussion.

The next morning was no different from the previous ones. We lazily rose from the floor, ate breakfast, hung around the house a bit, and headed for town. However, once we got off the bus at the bus stand, we headed for Stinson's Photo Studio. I asked Gautam, "Why are we going in here?"

He replied, "You are going to get your photo taken for your passport."

"What passport?" I inquired.

He looked at me, smiled, and said, "You are going to America."

I was dumbfounded. I looked at him and said, "Stop lying to me."

Len did not understand our conversation, but smiled and said, "Go take your picture." He placed his hand on my shoulder and asked, "Do you want to go to school in America?"

I was speechless and thought to myself, "America, me a twelve-year-old barefoot island boy in such a dreamland."

I figured Len and Gautam were playing with me, and my picture was being taken so Len could take one back with him. The photographer informed Gautam that he could pick up the picture in three days. We left the photo studio and walked the usual route over the canal past Morris Hedstrom Department Store toward GPH. Our next stop was the immigration office to pick up an application for my passport. Now I knew they were not joking. I was ecstatic and afraid. America. All I knew was what I saw in the movies: cowboys, Indians, big buildings, lots of cars, wide roads, and people who were all white and spoke too fast with funny accents. In my excitement and fear, my eyes became filled with water. My brother looked at me and asked, "What's wrong?"

"Nothing," I replied and kept walking.

On the way home, Len and my brother chatted, occasionally pointing at our friends in their trench coats. I walked quietly, trying to envision myself in America. We were a little late coming home. My father and uncle were already there. They were standing on the porch waiting for our arrival. As soon as we approached the house, Gautam said, "Well, we took the photo and picked up the application." Now I was sure that a plan had been laid for me to go to America.

The evening was quite warm, so even the children were sitting on the porch listening to stories and chatting. During the usual conversation, bhai looked at me and said, "Len wants to take you to America and educate you. You are a smart boy, and if you stay in Fiji, you would not be able to go to college."

I was sitting next to Len. He put his hand on my leg and assured me that I would enjoy Glendale, his hometown. "There are many young people your age to play with in the neighborhood." I smiled and nodded my head. A decision had already been made, and if I backed out, it would be a disgrace to the family and hurt bhai's pride.

Len was now starting his third week in Fiji. My passport was almost finished, and the only thing left to do was obtain a visa. Well, the American Consulate did not want to grant me a tourist or foreign student visa. They stated that it was highly irregular for a white person to sponsor a boy from the Islands, let alone a brown boy. Hearing this, Len lost his cool. He began cussing at the workers at the consulate office. "You white bastards, you have no right denying this boy a visa." He also used numerous other sentences laced with profanity. Len's anger lasted for quite some time, and he continued using many words that I could not understand, but I knew that these words had some deep meanings.

It wasn't until I had been in the United States for a while that I found out that the U.S. government thought of Len as a Communist and did not want him to indoctrinate me into his way of thinking. Another reason why they did not want to grant me a visa was that the United States did not readily allow black and brown people into the country. In 1962, there was no civil rights law. The third reason for the denial was that the city in which Len lived, Glendale, was an "all-white city." Anyone who was not white had to leave the city by sunset. Those non-whites that remained in the city after 6:00 PM were picked up by the police and dropped at the Los Angeles city boundary or spent the night in jail. Therefore, the school district did not want to send the necessary papers that would have qualified me for a visa.

The word of my leaving quickly spread throughout the community and other parts of the island. People began to address me as the "American kid." I was checked out of school, and amma and Gautam took me to the tailor for a new pair of long pants and to shop for new clothes and my first pair of shoes. Hundreds of people were dropping by to congratulate me, though some among the visitors chose to curse my parents for sending me. They were shouting that my parents had sold me to a white man and that America was an evil place. (By the way, some of those very same people now reside in the United States thanks to my father's ability to find sponsorship for them.)

The frenzy of my leaving and Len staying with us created a carnival-like atmosphere around our house every day. I was caught up in the hype and began to look forward to the departure date. I was the envy of my friends and the top kid in town. The commotion died when two days before our departure, we were informed that there was a delay in some paperwork and a visa could not be issued. Len knew the reason for the denial, so he informed my family that he had to go back to work and would make sure that I received a visa shortly. On the day of Len's departure, our whole extended family made a long trip to the airport to bid farewell to someone who had become a member of the family. As we said goodbye, Len had tears in his eyes. He hugged each member of the family and literally picked me up off the ground. We all cried as he walked around the corner and disappeared.

Although Len had disappeared from sight, nobody wanted to leave the airport. Everyone wanted to stay and watch the plane take off, a Pan American 707 jet. We all stood outside and watched the plane as its engines hummed and the plane began to move slowly. We waved, knowing that Len was looking out the window doing the same. Gautam looked over at three people wearing trench coats and made a comment to the effect of, "The vultures are still hovering while the dove flies away."

The ride home seemed to take forever. About forty of us were on the bus. Most of the people were sleeping during the ride back. I sat in the back with my brothers and cousins. There was an eerie quietness all around. After a while, we all fell asleep. When I awoke, the bus was making its way through the narrow streets toward our house. As soon as the bus stopped in front of the house, I dashed out, went straight into the house, and lay down on the bed in which Len used to sleep.

I began to visualize the inside of an airplane. I had never seen an airplane from up close, let alone being inside one. My mind wandered in various directions. Although there were people in the room talking, I felt all alone. In fact, I even felt a sense of fear run through me. I quickly opened my eyes, jumped out of bed, and walked outside. The air was warm, but I felt a sudden chill go through my body. My cousins and some of the neighborhood children were playing hide and seek. They invited me to join them, but I had no desire to play or speak with anyone.

Bhai was a man of few words and rarely showed his affection openly. He was the master of the house and the extended family. When he came home, he took a shower. His tea had to be ready soon after he came out of the shower. The children had to address him with respect and make no unnecessary noise. He had been watching my actions since our return from seeing Len off at the airport. When he saw me sulking instead of playing, he approached me, put his hand on my head, and simply stated, "Don't worry, my son, you will be going to America soon."

The next morning was strange. My brother Gautam went back to work. Len was gone, and I found myself all alone with nothing to do. After everyone had left for work and school, I asked my mother what I was supposed to do now that I was not going to America. She responded, "Go to school."

"But someone has to take and enroll me. I can't walk into the classroom and act like nothing has happened. I haven't been to school in a month."

The next morning, Gautam took me back to school. It was a humiliating feeling walking through the school watching children and adults alike pointing at me and whispering to each other. As I walked into the classroom, I could feel the uneasiness on the part of the students. After all, most of the students had been my pals since the first grade. Nevertheless, heads turned as I walked to the front of the room. The teacher looked at me and told me what seat to take. Some of my friends shouted, "Welcome back." Some students laughed and whispered to each other. Maybe I was being too sensitive and paranoid.

During the lunch break, some of the older students teased me by calling to me and asking, "How was America? Why did you come back so soon?" Some students even spoke to me in English, making fun of the fact that I was supposed to be in America. Well, I could not take it anymore and had to punch out a few of the kids. I was a good fighter, and one of the toughest boys in the whole school, Ashraf, was my best friend. When a couple of boys tried to gang up on me, my friend beat the living daylights out of them. He let all the kids know that if anyone teased me, they would receive a good hiding from him.

If ever there was a low point in my life, this was the moment. Because of the big excitement surrounding my journey to the "Promised Land" America, everyone put me on a pedestal. Now that the bubble had burst, I was looked upon as being a failure and a disappointment to everyone. In essence, I was being crucified. It came to light that the entire community was angry with me for somehow letting them down. They displayed their anger and disappointment through the name calling and teasing. I could not understand why the people behaved in such a manner. I went home and cried. I wished that I could leave and never come back.

Despite the degradation, I persevered. I resumed my old routine of going to school, playing soccer, and hanging out with some of my close friends. However, things were not the same. I had lost interest in many of the activities that had been exciting before. I went through the motions in the classroom and daydreamed about getting out of Fiji. The beauty that was Fiji was now tainted. What I deemed as being the essence of beauty of the Islands now became the object of my disdain. I began to question everything. Why did everyone have to know that I was going to America? Was I being punished by the higher beings that the religions were talking about? I could not answer these questions, but one thing I did know was that this was not something a thirteen-year-old boy was supposed to suffer through.

Almost a year had passed since Len's departure. In the midst of my agony, a letter arrived from America. Len wrote that he had spoken with the local school board, the governor of California, and several of the lawmakers to secure a visa for me. The letter was very optimistic. I, on the other hand, did not care. I wanted to settle into a life of fishing and enjoying my summer vacation. In Fiji, the summer vacation is during the months of December and January. Around Christmas, we had big gatherings with relatives. In the Islands, we did not exchange gifts, but we gathered with other families for parties that lasted a few days.

My father had a different plan for me during my summer vacation. He wanted me to work. I had no intention of working. All I wanted to do was hang out and fish. One day when I came home from fishing, my father took the fish, threw it into the street, and told me to get out there and get a job if I wanted to go back to school. I told him that I was sick and tired of working, and I wanted to have some fun. He became irate and hit me. He was already upset about something, and all I did was exacerbate the situation. I ran away, yelling at him and telling him that this was the last time he was going to hit me because I was going to go far away. I ran crying all the way to the riverbank where I usually fished. Instead of fishing, I just sat there looking into the water and crying. I was feeling sorry for myself and actually cursed the day I met Len. After all, if I hadn't met Len, I would not be experiencing any of these problems.

# Chapter Six:
# Leaving Home: A Journey to the Unknown

All of a sudden, my life and the lives of those around me took a turn in a different direction. Plans were being made to ascertain the best time to send me. Len had bought a ticket for me to fly on TEAL (Tasman Empire Airways Limited), an Australian airline that flew in and out of Fiji once a week. The only other airline that flew into Fiji was PAA (Pan American Airways). My brother and I went to the TEAL office in Suva and inquired about the next few flights to the United States. After much deliberation, I was booked on a flight leaving on February 11, 1962. We had two weeks to get my injections, medical exam, and all the legal papers necessary to depart Fiji.

My mother wanted to buy me some clothes, so I accompanied her on several shopping trips. Since this was Fiji's rainy season, it rained for two straight weeks. My mom and I braved the rainy weather and shopped. Occasionally, I got drenched as I ran back and forth from place to place. Our house again became filled with visitors. Every day and night, people were dropping by to congratulate me and to see if the grapevine about my impending departure for America was true or if this was another episode of the story. My friends were sad to see me leave; we had been together since childhood. Although the ambience around the house clearly reflected my impending departure, there was something unrealistic about the entire scenario. After all, whoever heard of a thirteen-year-old boy from a remote South Pacific island leaving his happy home and going away to America to live with a strange family?

The day before my journey, at least a hundred friends and relatives gathered at the house. Yes, the rumor had become a reality; the little boy was leaving. Food was being cooked outside on the open fire; people were sitting on the chatai exchanging stories. There was a festive and yet somber atmosphere. I was feeling sick. I don't know if the illness was psychosomatic, but my head hurt, I could barely breathe, and I felt like going to sleep and not waking up.

Hardly anybody in our immediate and extended family went to sleep that night. The environment was that of a wake. Preparations were being made for the long bus ride to the airport. The women were busy preparing food for the approximately fifty people who were coming to see me off at the airport.

When I woke up around 8:00 AM, there was a bus parked in front of the house and people were gathering to board the bus. Amma told me to take a shower, brush my teeth, and get dressed because it was almost time to leave. I was in a state of delirium. My head was still hurting, and I had the sniffles. However, I gained my composure and quickly walked to the bathroom.

Gautam had already taken my bag and placed it on the bus. On my way to board the bus, I was hugged and kissed by what appeared to be the entire island community. Many of the people were crying. Even my tough friend Ashraf, who had never shed a tear, began crying as he gave me a hug. Another friend grabbed me and said, "I cannot believe you are leaving us; don't forget us." I had tears in my eyes, but I did not want to cry. As I climbed on to the bus and looked back, I realized that I might never see some of these people again. Tears began to stream down my cheeks. There was nothing I could do to prevent the tears or the inexplicable feeling in the pit of my stomach.

The bus began to slowly pull away amidst shouts of "Goodbye," "Be good," "God bless you," "We love you," and "Don't forget to write." I stood up and waved profusely. Within seconds, my house disappeared from sight. While I was looking back and waving goodbye, my heart skipped a beat. Little by little, the familiar landscape began to disappear. Now I was convinced that my journey was taking me away from my home and family to a place that I had only imagined in my dreams.

All I knew was that it would be a long time before I gazed upon these familiar surroundings again. The bus roared past the river where I regularly went fishing. I waved goodbye to the river that had given me so much pleasure. In a short time, we were on the dusty gravel road headed to the airport. A few people had already fallen asleep. I kept my eyes open, enjoying the beauty of the land. The sun was shining, and the clear blue sky gave the ocean a deep-blue image. Along the way, I waved and shouted bula at villagers, people fishing along the riverbanks, and just about anyone I saw.

We had been traveling on the dusty, winding road for about four hours. Bhai asked the driver to find a place to stop for lunch. The bus driver stopped at a beautiful, serene area along the beach under hundreds of coconut trees. Everyone exited the bus rather hurriedly. They wanted to stretch their legs and walk on the white sandy beach. Mats were brought out and laid on the ground. The food was placed on the mats, and people served themselves buffet style. Some of us climbed the coconut trees for our favorite drink, coconut water. I ate a sandwich, drank my water, and ran to dip my feet in the warm, blue ocean for the last time. Walking along the ocean, swimming, and/or just sitting and watching the water brought about a peaceful feeling. I must have been standing there a long time daydreaming because the next thing I noticed was Gautam calling me to get on the bus.

Back on the bus, the people appeared to be relaxed and were chattering away. They were talking to me, to each other, and shouting to others from the back to the front of the bus. I guess the picnic gave everyone a burst of energy. Suddenly, I saw a sign that said, "Nadi, 20 miles." My heart skipped a beat. In about forty-five minutes, the bus would be pulling into the airport. I looked over at my brother Gautam and whispered, "I am afraid." He held my hand and told me not to worry. He said he wished he were going. After all, this was an opportunity of a lifetime that individuals rarely received. I said, "I know, but I feel sick and my stomach hurts."

He smiled and said, "The aches are caused by your fears. You are a big boy, and you can handle anything."

Gautam continued to reassure me that my journey to America would be great and that after I received my education, I could do anything. His attempts to comfort me actually made me feel worse, since it only reminded me of how much I was going to miss him and the rest of the family. I looked out the window and saw that we were passing through Nadi Town. Suddenly, I saw a sign saying, "Nadi Airport 5 miles." Another chill passed through my body. Then a sign, "Airport traffic keep left," came into view. People began to straighten up, pointing at the big 707 jet that came into view.

The plane had come from Sydney, Australia. We all climbed out of the bus and proceeded to the ticket counter. The airport was not crowded; there were only a few people milling around. Bhai, kaka, and Gautam accompanied me to the counter. I felt self-conscious and had a difficult time walking in my first pair of long pants and shoes.

The lady at the counter looked through the paperwork and asked, "Who is meeting you in Los Angeles?" Gautam gave her a piece of paper with Len's name, home telephone number, and address. He informed the attendant that I was not feeling well. She smiled and said to my family, "Do not worry; we will take good care of him."

As we walked back to where the family was waiting, amma grabbed me and began to cry loudly. She had been holding her emotions in check, but now that the time to leave was only minutes away, she could no longer contain herself. My mother's outburst created a chain reaction. Within seconds, almost everyone, young and old, was crying. Of course, I could not keep my composure, and tears began to flow freely from my welted watery eyes.

Saying goodbye became extremely difficult. Each person held me for a while, giving me advice and telling me to be careful. Suddenly, an announcement came over the loudspeaker for passenger Lal to please board the plane. The entire crowd slowly moved toward the gate. In those days, people could walk as close as thirty yards to the plane. As I inched toward the gate, I grabbed my uncle and began to cry. Hugging me, he assured me that everything would be fine. He was crying, as was Gautam; and for the first time in my life, I saw a sight that I never thought I would see. My father's eyes filled with tears as he hugged me and gave me his blessings.

Climbing the stairs to the entrance of the plane, I tripped twice because I was not used to wearing shoes. When I reached the top of the stairs, just before entering, I turned and waved to a group of people that I would not see for a long time. The attendant smiled at me and said, "I understand you are sad and afraid to leave your family. We," she pointed at the other attendants, "are here to make sure that you are comfortable. If you need anything, just press the button, and one of us will help you."

I really did not understand what she had said, but I smiled and stepped into the plane. Another attendant came and escorted me to my seat. She put the seatbelt on me and said, "Do not be afraid, just relax." I looked out the window and saw everyone waving. I waved back, hoping that they would see me. All of a sudden, the doors of the plane closed, and the pilot advised everyone to sit down for takeoff. I felt the plane move. My brothers, cousins, and some of my friends were running to keep up with the plane as it moved. An abundance of tears flowed down my cheeks as the plane roared its engines and moved faster and faster.

I was terrified. I had never seen a plane on the ground before, let alone sat in one that was preparing to fly. In my fear, I closed my eyes as the plane began to climb into the sky. When I opened my eyes, the plane was diagonal and still climbing. There was complete silence all around me except for the loud noise of my heartbeat. This object was too heavy to stay in the sky. How can it remain up here? What happens if the plane falls? These questions kept running through my mind.

When the plane straightened, a voice came out of the roof. The person identified himself as the pilot and announced that he was turning off the "fasten seatbelt" sign, and passengers were free to move around the cabin if they wished. I looked around to see where the sound was coming from. Then I saw the speaker above the seat, right next to the small lights. An attendant came and asked if I wanted something to drink. I ordered a ginger ale. Later, she brought me some food, but I told her that I was feeling sick and did not feel like eating. "Would you like to lie down and go to sleep?" she asked.

I smiled and replied, "Yes."

The attendant escorted me to another area where there were three empty seats. I was given a blanket and a pillow, and the armrests were raised so I could sleep in comfort. I thanked the attendant for her kindness, took off my uncomfortable shoes, and made an effort to sleep. However, as soon as I closed my eyes, images of people crying and members of the family running to keep up with the plane flashed through my brain. Tears began to drip down my cheeks. I turned over and buried my face in the pillow. Visions of my relatives and friends kept going through my mind.

No matter what I did, I could not stop crying or thinking about being all alone.

I must have cried myself to sleep, because when I opened my eyes, the passengers were being served breakfast. I sat up and asked the attendant, "How long before we arrive in America?"

She replied, "We are about to land in Honolulu."

I asked for a piece of toast and some tea. As I was eating, I looked out of the window and saw nothing but clouds. Of course, I had no idea where we were or in what direction we were flying. Tears again began to fill my eyes. Then I heard a voice, "Can I get you something more to drink?" It was the flight attendant who was extremely conscientious about me. I smiled, said no, and lay down.

I could feel the plane slowing and reducing its elevation. The pilot informed us that we were approaching Honolulu International Airport and would be landing soon and that everyone had to put on their seatbelts. As the plane inched toward the terminal, I could see the landscape dotted with beautiful coconut trees and some tall buildings. This looked just like Fiji. The pilot informed us that we would be at the terminal for two hours and that we were to disembark so the plane could be cleaned.

I was the last passenger to get off the plane. As I walked out, I heard someone call my name. I turned around and saw a lady holding a flower lei and walking toward me. She placed the lei around my neck, gave me a kiss, and said, "Aloha! Welcome to Hawaii." I was shocked. She introduced herself as Carolyn, a friend of Len's. She then turned and introduced me to her son, who was about my age, and her daughter, perhaps a year or so younger than I. I was so thrilled to have someone meet me at this strange airport. Carolyn explained that Len had written to her and asked her to meet me at the airport.

Since I was the only island boy getting out of the plane, it was not too difficult for Carolyn to pick me out from the rest of the passengers. They bought me some pineapple juice and showed me around the airport. We talked about Hawaii and Fiji. Carl, the son, was very pleasant and friendly. He knew that I had a limited ability to speak English, so he spoke slowly and used gestures. I immediately fell in love with Hawaii and its beautiful people.

The Thompson family stayed with me until the plane was ready to depart. They assured me that Len would be at the Los Angeles Airport waiting. As bid farewell, I thanked them for their kindness and slowly boarded the plane.

As the plane was taxiing on the runway, I looked back and waved goodbye to a family that had embraced me although they didn't even know me. I knew that I would definitely see them again. I was congested, so I had a difficult time breathing and at times found myself coughing. Anyhow, I managed to fall asleep. The next thing I remember is the attendant waking me and telling me that we had arrived. I sat up, looked out the window, and saw that we were on the ground. I straightened my clothes and picked up my little bag, and the attendant escorted me down the aisle toward the door.

# Chapter Seven: America the Enchanted Land

Stepping out of the plane and looking around, all I could see was a strange, dark, and dreary place. There were no coconut or mango trees, just buildings. It was drizzling. The attendant held my hand and quickly led me into the terminal. There was a big sign that read, "Welcome to Los Angeles." I looked around in the crowd to find Len but could not see him. Fear gripped me. What if nobody was here? I kept looking through the crowd and finally spotted Len in his familiar baseball cap and with a smile. He waved at me, and I waved back, feeling relieved that I was not abandoned.

After clearing immigration, I ran up and gave Len a hug. We both were truly ecstatic about seeing each other. He introduced me to his daughter, Shirley; son-in-law, Gordon; and his thirteen-year-old nephew, Warren. They greeted me with warm, pleasant handshakes. Len asked me about the flight, my family, and if I had met the Thompsons in Honolulu. I cheerfully shared all the information about my departure from Nadi and the great time I had with the Thompsons.

We made our way through the crowd to the baggage claim area. I had only brought one bag, since there really wasn't much I could bring except for a few gifts. Gordon kept a vigilant watch and grabbed my bag as soon as it came off the ramp.

Los Angeles Airport was not very big or crowded in February 1962. I was amazed to find out that it was Sunday afternoon. How could I leave Sunday night from Fiji and arrive in Los Angeles on Sunday afternoon? I was too embarrassed to ask anyone. Curiosity got the best of me and finally I did ask Len, and he explained the international dateline and how and why I had gained a day. Well, my American education had already commenced, and I had not yet left the airport.

As we stepped outside into the damp weather, Warren turned to me and said, "It has been raining for over a week." I had never experienced cold weather like this. Of course, it was 60 degrees, but for an island boy who had never experienced anything below 75 degrees, this was cold. We walked to the parking lot, and Gordon headed toward a 1959 green Chevrolet. Len, Warren, and I sat in the back seat. All four of them were asking me questions and carrying on a conversation. I did not understand the majority of their conversation or their questions. However, I always answered with a smile. Eventually, they all realized that they would have to use gestures and concrete objects to communicate, or they would just get a cute smile from my pearly white teeth.

I was amazed at the number of cars on the streets. Moreover, I was totally taken by the width of the streets. I could not believe what I was seeing: three cars going one way, and three coming the other way. In Fiji, our main highway was a gravel road with only one lane going each way. Nevertheless, I was in for another surprise. Gordon drove onto a street where we traveled at a great speed. I quickly learned that this road, where there were no lights and cars traveled 65 miles per hour, was known as a freeway.

The cars seemed to be flying on the freeway. I had never seen an automobile move so fast in my life. On the freeway, the cars darted in and out of lanes while moving at such high speeds. Len looked at me and said, "Don't be afraid. On the freeway, you must drive fast or people will start honking and getting upset." In Fiji, we did not have very many cars on the road. We used to play a game counting the number of cars that would travel on the main highway in an hour. I realized that in America there were too many cars to count.

The ride appeared endless. We traveled one way and then another from freeway to freeway. One thing I did know was that we were headed for 800 Windsor Road in Glendale. After all, my family had written many letters to that address over the last three years. All of a sudden, the cars appeared to be slowing. I looked ahead to see what was happening. The road had narrowed, and three lanes had become one. Gordon looked back and informed Len that because of the rain, everyone was taking it easy around the off ramp. Then I saw a sign saying, "Glendale." I knew we had arrived or at least were not too far away from the house.

Gordon turned onto a street called Colorado Boulevard and then onto Brand Boulevard. (These two streets became very familiar to me in the future.) We were coming to a stop in front of what appeared to be a theater. Gordon stopped the car and said, "Here we are." I wondered why we were going to see a film at this time. I was hungry, tired, and not feeling too well. However, I smiled and stepped out of the car.

Len looked at me and said, "I bet you are hungry."

I knew what hungry meant and quickly replied, "Yes." We walked past the movie theater and into a cafeteria. It was nice and warm inside. The cafeteria was huge with many tables and a food counter that stretched on forever. This was the biggest eating place I had ever seen. People were talking, dishes were clanging, and the smell of food was intoxicating. My dilemma was that I did not know what to eat. I got in line behind Warren. I figured I would follow his lead and pick some of the same kind of food.

Despite wanting to follow Warren's lead, I did not pick up anything because nothing appealed to me. I saw some chicken soup and decided it was safe to have bread, soup, and maybe a piece of chicken. Since it was cold, I wanted some tea to drink. I saw Warren pick up a pot of what I thought was tea and emulated him. Much to my disappointment, Warren had picked up a small pot of coffee. I had never drunk coffee and did not like the taste. Additionally, the soup tasted awful, and the chicken had a dreadful smell; in fact, all the food had a strange smell.

It was not until a week or so later, when Sylvia and Len asked me why I did not eat my meat that I explained to them that the food had a strange odor that made me want to vomit. There I was, hungry yet unable to eat anything because of the taste and smell. I put some butter and jam on my bread and made that my dinner.

Warren had played a trick on me about the coffee. After I followed his lead, he put back his coffee. I was too ashamed to say anything, and the others figured that because of my being ill, I did not want to eat. This was my first meal in America, but I was too naïve to know what to choose and too proud to ask.

One peculiar incident happened while we were in line getting our food. Two elderly white ladies got in line behind us; I turned around, smiled, and nodded my head. They looked at me, took their trays, and walked away. I could not understand what I had done that was wrong. The ladies muttered something and disappeared from sight. When we walked toward our table, I felt as if every eye in the cafeteria was aimed toward us. "Why is everyone looking at us?" I asked Len.

He answered, "These people have never seen anyone from the island so they are interested in you." Little did I know that they were wondering what a dark boy was doing in their city and at their restaurant.

Back then I didn't know anything about the segregation laws of the United States and of individual cities and states. It was difficult to imagine that a country such as America had laws that condoned the mistreatment of non-whites. This was 1962, and the Civil Rights Bill granting non-whites equal rights was not signed into law by President Lyndon Johnson until 1964.

Glendale had a Sunset Rule, a city law that stated that non-whites could not be in the city after sunset. So, all the cleaning ladies, car washers, gardeners, and restaurant workers who were either Latino or black had to get out of town by dusk. Those who did not leave the city were picked up by the police and were dropped at San Fernando Road, the Los Angeles city boundary. Later in life, I also learned that Glendale was the home of the right-wing organization the John Birch Society. The old joke used to be, "How do you get to Glendale? Just keep turning right."

I looked outside and saw that nightfall had come. The rain was still falling. We had finished our meal, and it was time to make our way home. Now I would finally get to see the address to which my letters were delivered. Gordon drove down Brand Boulevard; it was a busy street with many businesses and restaurants. He then made a left on Windsor Road. Windsor Road was a street with neatly trimmed trees and manicured lawns. Gordon turned the car into a driveway that was long with three homes on the lot. There was a nice house in the front, a small house in the middle, and Len's house at the end of the driveway with a detached garage. Now I knew why the address was 800 B East Windsor Road. In front of the house was a beautiful lawn with a nice big tree at one end. The house was light green with white trim with a porch that had two chairs on it. I was excited to have finally arrived.

Warren stepped out of the car and ran into the house. Shirley called to me, "Come on, Dhyan; we are home." I followed Len into the house. I was amazed at the size of the house. The family room and kitchen were the size of our entire house in Fiji. By American standards, this two-bedroom house was just an ordinary place. To me, this was a mansion.

Len introduced me to his niece Sylvia, Warren's mother, and her daughters, Susan, Jo Ann, and Sherry. They were all in elementary school. Sylvia appeared to be a very loving person. She extended her arm, shook my hand, and welcomed me to the family and the United States. "How was your trip?" she asked. "You must be tired from such a long plane ride." Gordon took my bag and placed it in one of the bedrooms. Sylvia and the three girls occupied one bedroom, Len and Warren the other. I surmised that I would be joining Len and Warren.

The girls had been watching a box that had moving pictures like a film theater. They called this thing a television. How amazing, a theater right in the house. I looked at this for a minute and figured they had some kind of a projector somewhere. Shirley and Gordon said it was getting late, and they were going home. They said they would see me tomorrow.

I was not feeling well, so I bid good night to everyone and went into Len's room. He had a big king-sized bed in there and a twin bed. The room had a desk, a closet, a chest of drawers, and a file cabinet. Len pointed to the twin bed. "That's your bed; you can go to sleep anytime." I didn't need any further encouragement. Soon after changing my clothes, I climbed into the warm, soft bed and fell asleep.

When I woke up, it was ten the next morning. I must have slept for over twelve hours. I knew the others were already up, because I could hear people talking. I slowly climbed out of bed and went to the bathroom. After brushing my teeth and changing clothes, I went into the family room, where Sylvia and Len were sitting enjoying their coffee. They spoke at the same time, "Good morning. You must have had a great sleep." As usual, I didn't understand everything that was said, so I smiled and nodded my head.

Sylvia asked, "Would you like some toast and eggs?"

"Yes, thank you," I replied.

I sat down with Len and stared at the outside surroundings for a while. Len put his hand on my shoulder and said, "Today is a holiday, Lincoln's Birthday. You do not have to go to school." He called Warren and reminded him that we would go shopping for clothes for me after we were through eating breakfast. Sylvia brought me fried eggs, toast, a glass of orange juice, and milk. I had never had breakfast like this, what a treat. When I took a bite of the bread, it had a strange taste, and the cold milk was watery. In Fiji, our bread was always fresh and delivered by the bakery truck, and the milk was fresh from the farm. I guess food in America tasted funny because it was frozen for a long time. Not having refrigeration in Fiji required that all food items were bought fresh for same-day use or taken out of one's personal vegetable garden.

After breakfast, Warren, Len, and I went to the shops in Glendale. It was cloudy, with a slight breeze that made my bones shiver, and it was still drizzling. We drove on Brand Boulevard again to get to the section with all the stores. Most of the stores were closed because of the holiday. We found JCPenney to be open. Len suggested that we buy a couple items and wait until the following weekend to buy the rest of the clothes for me. Walking into the store was like something one sees in a movie: a big store with rows and rows of clothes. I didn't think anything like this existed. Warren walked right over to the boys' section and pointed to some shirts and jeans that I could wear to school.

After trying on several shirts and pants, I picked the two pairs of pants and three shirts that I liked and a jacket. Len paid for the clothes, and we were out of the store. Len drove around the town to show me some sights and stopped in front of Roosevelt Junior High School. He looked at me and pointed out that this was the school I was going to attend. Warren smiled and uttered, "You'll like it here." I stared at the school through the raindrops and thought to myself, what a huge building. Len slowly drove around the corner to the area where the grass field and the gym were located. By this time, I was getting used to looking at things that were bigger than what I could imagine. I began to realize that everything in America was big.

It was late in the afternoon when we came back to the house. I was cold and tired. As soon as we entered the house, I turned on the television and lay down on the couch. A cowboy movie, my favorite, was playing. I had thought that America was like movies with cowboys roaming, ranchers, and people riding horses in the streets.

Len had gone to take a nap, and Warren said he was going to see a friend. So when nobody was around, I looked behind the television to see how the pictures were coming to the screen. I looked all around the set, in the walls, and even throughout the family room, but could not find the source of the images on the screen. America had already made an impression on me, but this was truly perplexing. Finally, I lay down on the couch, watched the movie, and fell asleep.

When the rain subsided, I decided to venture outside and walk around the streets to familiarize myself with the surroundings. Windsor Road, as was most of the city of Glendale, was dotted with single-family homes, big backyards, and beautiful lawns in front. The entire city was surrounded by hills. It was beautiful to see the clouds hanging over the green hills with the sun attempting to break through. I did not walk too far because I was afraid I would get lost and not be able to find my way home.

Glendale is nestled in the foothills of the San Gabriel Mountains. In 1962, it was a quaint little city, a suburb of the larger city of Los Angeles. The streets were wide and clean. The main street, Brand Boulevard, was lined with retail and specialty stores. The tallest building was five stories high. There were a few small factories on the outskirts of town. On the northwest corner of the city, by the Los Angeles River (which was cemented and had very little water flowing), was a dairy farm. A few blocks from the dairy farm were horse-riding stables. Yes, it was 1962, and Glendale was a city that was growing, but it still maintained some country atmosphere.

# Chapter Eight: First Day of School

"Wake up; it is seven, and you have to get ready to go to school."
I opened my eyes and saw Len standing over me with his hand on my
shoulder. "You are a hard one to wake," he said. It was cold outside, and I
wanted to stay underneath the nice warm blanket. Just then, Warren came
in with a toothbrush in his mouth gesturing to me to get out of bed. Slowly
and reluctantly, I dragged myself out of bed. Sylvia was already cooking
breakfast, but the girls were still sleeping. Since they were in elementary
school, which began later than the junior high school, they could sleep a
little longer. I brushed my teeth and jumped into the shower.

After nearly burning myself, I discovered that there was hot water
coming out of the faucet. I screamed, and Len came in to see what was
wrong. He explained to me about the hot and cold water faucets and how
to regulate them. The only time warm water came out of the faucet in Fiji
was during the hot tropical days. There was only one knob; we turned it on
and took a shower. Americans were geniuses; they made hot water come
out of the pipes. Warren was totally amused at my predicament and was
laughing when I came out of the bathroom.

Sylvia and Len accompanied me to school to register me and make
sure that I was placed in the appropriate classes. While Len and Sylvia

were completing the necessary forms for enrollment, I looked around. It was astonishing to see such a large number of students and the size of the hallways.

Everyone in the offices knew Sylvia because she was the president of the Parent Teachers Association (PTA). The principal, assistant principal, and other adults dropped in to say hello to us and welcomed me to the school. Len told me that because of her involvement in the school, Sylvia was much respected in the school community. No wonder everyone was so nice to us.

A counselor came in and conferred with us regarding the classes that I needed to take in order to fulfill the requirements for graduation from junior high school. All the paperwork was done, and Sylvia and Len bid me good luck and departed.

Warren had already gone to his class. I was not placed in the same classes as Warren because he was in the honors classes, whereas I was placed in the lower-level classes. Students referred to these as dumbbell classes. All of a sudden, I felt a strange sensation; fear gripped me. I was afraid of what was coming next. I sat silently in the office wondering what was going to happen. A student walked in and was introduced to me as my guide. She was very cordial and motioned to me to follow her. I smiled and followed my guide down the long hallway, out the door, and into another building.

Upon entering the classroom, my guide handed the teacher a paper, and turned to me and said, "Wait for me when the class is over." The teacher stopped lecturing, introduced me to the class, and showed me a seat that would be my assigned seat for the rest of the year. I glanced at the class, then the teacher, and finally realized that everyone I had met since my arrival in America looked the same. They were all white. Of course, I knew this was a white country, but I wondered if there was anyone who looked like me.

The teacher resumed her lecturing. She was talking so fast that I could only understand a few of her words. While sitting in class, my mind began to wander to thoughts about home. What was everyone doing? What was happening at my old school in Samabula? Before I knew it, tears began to roll down my cheeks. I tried to conceal my crying, but was unable to control this involuntary flowing of water from my eyes. I had no idea what the teacher was saying, except that it was something about American history.

In the midst of my daydream, a strange sound came out of the speaker in the classroom. When I looked up, all the students were gathering their belongings and dashing out the door. The teacher looked at me and said, "That was the bell. It's time for you to go to your next class." We did not have speakers, bells, or clocks in the classroom at Samabula Government School; the teacher told us what to do and when to do it. My guide appeared at the door, ready to take me to my next destination, a math class. It was slightly drizzling and cold. I wished I were back in Fiji with my friends playing in the warm sun. After second period, it was time for nutrition. I was taken to the cafeteria where I could purchase food and drinks.

A restaurant in a school; this was the ultimate. Back home, we only had a few restaurants in the entire town, but to have one in the school was beyond imagination. Even today, schools in Fiji do not have cafeterias or even machines in the schools. While standing there looking at the line, I caught a glimpse of Warren. He approached and asked, "Have you eaten anything?"

"No," I replied. "I am not hungry." I did, however, want a cup of hot chocolate because I was cold, but I was too ashamed to ask.

Warren introduced me to some of his friends. They were very curious about where I was from and the way I looked. One boy asked me if Fiji was in Africa and another asked, "Do you have houses and wear clothes in your country?"

I soon became aware of the stares I received from the adults and students. These stares were similar to the ones I received in the cafeteria, especially from the two women who walked out of the line. Some students shook my hand while others did not extend their hands. Most people in the school had never come in close contact with a dark person, so they were very curious, whereas others had various reasons, including racism, for their behaviors.

Since I did not understand much of the language, I was unaware of some of the comments made by a number of students. In essence, they were calling me derogatory names. Of course, the name-calling did not bother me because I didn't know what they were saying.

The last period of the day was physical education. I had no idea what this meant. We walked into this huge building with a clean, shiny floor, and basketball nets. All the boys were dressed in special uniforms, red shorts and white T-shirts. They all lined up in squads and answered when the teacher called their names. In Fiji, our sports time consisted of going in our regular clothes and participating in the sport that was in season. There were no special uniforms or buildings to play in.

A coach walked over and motioned to me to follow him to the office. He put my name in his roll book and said, "You have to buy the uniform from the student store and dress for gym tomorrow." He asked me if I had money, and I said yes. He motioned for one of the students to come over. He asked the student to take me to the student store so I could buy my clothes.

I thought I had seen everything until I saw the store. The number of items the student store was selling overwhelmed me. If I told the folks back home about this school, they would not believe me. This was a city, not a school. They even had machines that you could put money into and get an orange, an apple, or a soft drink of your choice.

I bought my clothes and headed back to the gym. The coach led me into a room that had lockers. He directed me to a locker and showed me how to use the combination to open the locker. His exact instructions were, "This is your locker. You are responsible for making sure that it is kept locked at all times and don't give your combination to anyone." So this was the place students came to change into their exercise clothes.

I looked around and saw that there were showers with hot and cold water and towels for each student. I could not wait to get back to the house and write a letter home to tell everyone about this incredible country and the phenomenal school that I was attending.

When school was over, Warren and I walked to the front and saw Len waiting for us. The chilly rain was falling sporadically. Len asked, "So, how was your first day?"

"It was great," I replied and proceeded to tell him about my experiences.

Len was kind enough to give us a ride on this cold, rainy day despite the fact that he had to go to work. He worked at a printing company in Los Angeles from 4:00 PM until 11:00 PM. As I walked into the house, I saw that the television was on, so I sat down on the chair and began to watch cartoons with the girls. I was thoroughly fascinated by television. What a great invention; a press of the button, and you have instant films coming through the wires.

After watching television for a while, I went into the bedroom and lay down on the bed. A strange feeling gripped me as I lay there looking at the ceiling. I realized that I was alone. It was difficult to communicate with people because of the language barrier. I began to cry and wished I were home in the comfort of my family and the familiar surroundings. If I were back home, I would be playing with my friends instead of being shut in a room by myself. I was lonely and homesick. That night, I cried myself to sleep.

# Chapter Nine:  Garcie: A Friend for Life

The next morning, it was the same routine. I really was not too excited about going to school. After all, I had no friends, the food tasted strange, and I did not understand most of what people were saying. The rest of the week was much the same, except that I made a few acquaintances.

On Friday, the counselor called me into his office and introduced me to person who was also from a different country and had skin and features that were not like the others in the school. His name was Manuel Garcia, and he had enrolled in the school the previous week. Manuel's family had just migrated from Peru, a country in South America. Like me, he did not speak English. I was pleased to meet Manuel and could see the feeling was mutual.

A student from the school newspaper came and took our picture while we pointed to our respective countries on the world globe. They wrote an article about us and placed our pictures on the front page of the school paper. After reading about our backgrounds, numerous students went out of their way to say hello to us. The students appeared to be friendlier toward us. Some even assisted us in the classes and outside during the breaks.

Garcie and I became instant friends. We met each other every morning and hung around together throughout the day. Little by little, our ability to converse in English improved, and we were able to communicate verbally instead of having to use gestures. Overall, most were very nice to us now. There were some students who made remarks to us that were belittling, but we ignored them.

We were popular in our physical education class because both of us were good runners and soccer players. Still, some students attempted to trip us on purpose when we ran or attempted to push us during games.

One day, when I was taking a shower after the physical education class, one boy came to me and yelled, "Nigger, move out of the shower; that's mine." I didn't know what that meant, so I kept washing my hair and face. The boy pushed me. All the other boys laughed. I was embarrassed, but I was not going to let this guy insult me. I turned around and punched him right in the mouth. He was shocked because he was not expecting me to respond in such a manner. As he attempted to hit me, I socked him in the stomach. The noise attracted the attention of the coach. He asked us to stop and to see him after we were dressed.

I walked into the coach's office, and he asked, "Why were you fighting?" I explained the whole story about how the fight had started.

He then asked the other boy what happened, and the boy gave his version of the story saying, "He started the fight for no reason," pointing at me. After the other boy was finished telling his side of the story, the coach asked me to leave. Later, I was told that the boy had received two swats from the coach for picking on me. Of course, this boy was very upset at me and blamed me for getting him in trouble.

After school, he and four of his friends were waiting for me around the corner of a building. As I walked by, they shouted, "Hey, black boy, jungle boy, show us how tough you are." They pushed me against the wall, and one of them hit me in the stomach. I fought back, but two of them held my arms. Unexpectedly, Garcie appeared and grabbed one of the boys, threw him to the ground, and kicked the other one. The two who were holding me let go of my arms, and I socked one of them on the right ear. Garcie and I began fighting like two individuals who were possessed. In our rage, we scared the bullies, and they ran.

We picked up our books and I asked, "Garcie, are you all right?"

"Fine," he replied. "How abut you?" I was bleeding from my mouth, but it was just a little cut. While walking, we began to brag about how we had simply kicked ass on five guys. I told Garcie about the incident in the shower and why these boys wanted to teach me a lesson.

Garcie was the quiet type, and I was more verbal and outgoing. He said that a couple of boys had made fun of his accent earlier, but he ignored them. We talked about our adventurous day during the walk home.

We decided that we were not going to let anyone make fun of us because we were different and that we would let our fists do the talking. Garcie asked me to come into his house and meet his mom. She was a nice lady who smiled, shook my hand, and asked Garcie to ask me if I wanted something to drink. Garcie had told her all about me and how I had left my family in Fiji and was living with Len and his family. She brought some chicken and rice for us to eat. At first, I did not want to eat, but this food smelled pleasant. With the first bite, I could taste a hint of spices and some other seasoning. Finally, I was eating food that did not smell or taste bad.

I was beginning to feel good about myself and about America. Now I had a friend who was experiencing the same problems as me and liked the same kinds of things. I invited Garcie to visit our house on a Saturday. He rode his bicycle to the house the following Saturday. I introduced him to Len and told him that sometimes I went to Garcie's house after school. Len was happy to see that I had a friend who appeared to be a very nice boy.

Since it was close to lunchtime, Len asked us if we wanted to go to Bob's Big Boy for lunch. We were thrilled because we had heard students at school talk about going to Bob's and having the Big Boy. This was our first time at Bob's, another new experience for me.

Bob's was the kind of place where you could drive up in your car, park, and a girl comes up to you and asks, "What would you like to eat?" She brought your food on a tray and hooked the tray to the door, and you sat right in the car and ate. However, we did not sit and eat in the car. We sat inside. Garcie and I both ordered a Big Boy, fries, and a cherry Coke. Len had soup and salad. We talked all through lunch. Len asked Garcie about his family, how many brothers and sisters he had, and how the family came to the United States.

Len liked Garcie and approved of him as a friend. After all, I could have befriended someone who was involved in antisocial behaviors or took drugs. Garcie and I hung around on weekends at the house or went to play on the school playground. We really became close friends. Of course, our survival depended on us looking out for one another. We were becoming popular at school and made some new American friends, especially in the physical education class.

In the gym class, the squad leaders were choosing members for the football teams. All students out of approximately 125 were chosen except for Garcie and I. Everyone figured we were stupid because we didn't say much and also because neither one of us had ever played American football. We both knew how to play the real football, which was called soccer in America.

The coach assigned us to different teams, much to the displeasure of the captains. I was assigned by my team's captain to rush the quarterback on offense and block on defense the few times I was in the game. When they did let me play, I was usually the first one chasing the quarterback.

However, I was not that good at blocking, because the big kids would always knock me down.

Before long, everybody realized that Garcie and I were fast and had some natural athletic abilities. To make ourselves better at this sport called football, Garcie bought a football, and we began throwing and catching the ball every chance we had. After a while, we could run down the field and catch the ball without stopping. Football was no different from soccer, except we used our hands instead of our feet to control the ball.

One day, I asked the captain to let me run down to catch the ball, and all the other guys on the team laughed. A team member looked at me and said, "You're lucky to be in the game, so shut up and block." The quarterback told me to line up at the end and run down as far as I could when the ball was hiked. As soon as the ball was hiked, I ran as fast as I could. The quarterback was being chased so he just threw the ball high in the air in my direction. I ran toward the middle, caught the ball, and ran to the touchdown line. My teammates were stunned. They knew I was fast, but they had no idea I could catch too.

When we were getting dressed in the locker room, Garcie came up to me and said he had heard about my big catch. He said he heard the boys talking about my moves. We just looked at each other and laughed.

# Chapter Ten: Me, a Celebrity

The fact that I was a thirteen-year-old from a remote island in the South Pacific living with an American family in Glendale and attending a neighborhood school gained the interest of the local newspaper, *Glendale News Press*. The paper contacted me and said that they were interested in writing an article about how I came to the country, my family back home, and the family with whom I was living. I gave them my home telephone number and told them that they had to speak with my guardian. They contacted Len and gained his permission to interview both of us.

After the article in the paper, various civic and religious groups in the community asked me to come and speak to their members. In the beginning, I was apprehensive about speaking because of my accent and the fear of standing in front of all the strange people. I could not understand all the fuss being made over me until Len explained that most people did not even know where Fiji was let alone having seen someone from there. I was still afraid, but it became easier to express myself after the first few presentations.

The first test of my ability to speak in front of an audience occurred in my English class. The teacher wanted me to write an essay about my country and give an oral report. During the presentation, the students were very attentive. They had many questions for me. For instance, one student wanted to know what kind of food people ate and if they cooked the food.

Of course, the most often asked question was, "Can you say something in your language?" I was delighted to oblige by bursting out with "Bula," which stands for hello, goodbye, and other greetings in Fijian. Although the questions seemed bizarre, in retrospect, I understand that the only reference they had to Fiji was what they saw on the television and the pictures they saw in the *National Geographic* magazine.

Speaking in front of older audiences was especially pleasing. They would ask me questions to which I did not have answers. I quickly learned that I needed to have answers, or the people would be disappointed.

I remember once when I spoke in front of the PTA. I spoke about diving for coins when the ships came into the harbor, fishing with homemade spears, and catching crabs with my hands. The ladies were mesmerized by my stories. One lady stated that she had read that Fijians were cannibals. I responded by letting her know that I personally had never tasted human flesh, but did hear that the thigh was the best-tasting part of the body.

I took a special delight in telling the story about Udre Udre, the Fijian chief who was a devout cannibal and ate ninety-nine people. He eventually died of indigestion.

Everywhere I went in Glendale, people's curiosity about the Islands usually dominated their conversations with me. Most people had trouble pronouncing my name. They would call me Don, John, Dion, and even Diane. Even now, I receive mail addressed to Ms. Lal or receive telephone calls asking for Diane Lal. I would ask about the nature of the call and inform the party on the other side that she was not home.

My school acquaintances just began calling me Fiji, but some couldn't even get that correct and called me Fuji.

The island boy was a celebrity in the small town of Glendale, but ignorance was alive and well everywhere else. One weekend, we went to the desert. Len found a very nice hotel in Desert Hot Springs. He went to the clerk and asked for two rooms, one for Sylvia and the other for him,

Warren, and me. The desk clerk said he had two good rooms. He asked Len how many in the second room, and Len pointed to us. The clerk looked at me then turned to Len and said that he just realized they only had one room available. Len became very angry and asked to see the manager.

The manager repeated the same lie about not having another room available. It was apparent that the clerk had already briefed the manager about the situation. Back then, I was not aware of the underlying reason for their refusal to let us stay there. When I was older and more aware, I asked Len about the incidents at the hotel, in the cafeteria, and in the consulate's office in Fiji. He replied, "Those racist bastards did not want you because you were dark." I already had figured out what had happened, but wanted to hear it from Len.

That evening Len reluctantly drove home. He was angry, but above all, he was sorry that I had to face this bigotry from these ignorant people. When Len became angry, he yelled at the people and let them know precisely what he thought of them. I, on the other hand, not knowing what was going on, enjoyed the outings. I was puzzled as to why Len sometimes became so irate at people when we went to places. Every weekend, we went to visit a different part of Southern California.

Life in America for me was like a dream. In Fiji, we had no electricity, and the bathroom was outside. We took our showers under the stars. Here I had light at the flip of a switch; the bathroom was five steps from my bedroom, and the food was cooked inside on a stove instead of outside on the open fire. I had been in the country for four months; nevertheless, I continued to be flabbergasted by all the sights.

Notwithstanding everything I had seen, two things eluded me. I did not see streets paved with gold or trees with money on them. What people back in Fiji meant was that money was plentiful and easy to get in America. Because I was at an impressionable age and naïve, I truly believed that money grew on trees.

Despite the trips, all the comforts of life, and materialistic possessions, I was still unhappy. A number of times, Len found me crying in the bedroom. He would attempt to comfort me, but knew that I was lonely and homesick. One evening while I was lying in bed, I overheard Len speaking with Sylvia. He confided in her that he thought he had made a mistake by bringing me to the United States. He said he did not realize the negative impact leaving the family and home would have on me when he first discussed the idea with my father.

She said that she also was concerned about me, but reassured him that I would get over the homesickness. As they were talking, I felt my eyes filling with water. My mind wandered to thoughts of home. What were the family members doing? Did they know how miserable I was? A sudden chill ran through my body. I was afraid, but of what I did not know. That night, like many other nights, I cried myself to sleep.

Although I studied diligently and always completed my homework, I still received the mark of D in two of the subjects. Neither Len nor I were pleased with the two Ds; therefore, I went to summer school to remove the less-than-satisfactory marks. I enrolled in algebra and English for the summer.

Len bought me a bicycle to ride back and forth to school. I was ecstatic about having my own bike. No student in Samabula had a bike, and here I was with my very own Schwinn bicycle. I had Garcie take a few pictures of me on the bike and sent them home. In fact, we took photographs of all the places we visited, including Disneyland, and sent them home.

In retrospect, sending the pictures may have been a mistake because everyone in Fiji thought I was having the time of my life. The pictures combined with the descriptions of places I had visited added to the people's beliefs that the "streets were paved with gold and money grew on trees."

Well, I received a B in Algebra and a C in English during summer school. The marks were a result of my efforts and perseverance. After all, I was the top dog in my classes in Fiji and receiving Ds was embarrassing

We headed for a vacation at Yosemite National Park as soon as summer school was over. Yosemite is one of the most beautiful parks in the world. It is located in the mountains of Central California. Waterfalls and tall trees surround the valley. Wildlife such as bears, elks, and deer were plentiful. Len had rented two small cabins for two weeks. We drove to Yosemite in two cars, because there were eight of us. Driving through the winding roads, up and down hills, we came to a tunnel that was carved right in the mountain. It was strange driving through the tunnel. Len blew the car horn. The sound of the horn was loud, and it echoed through the tunnel.

Exiting the tunnel, we were treated with beautiful scenery. Beneath us was a lush, green valley with two gigantic waterfalls cascading down the mountainside. Len stopped the car so we could step out and appreciate the breathtaking view. I was overwhelmed at the magnificence before me. Never in my wildest dreams had I imagined such wilderness, mountains touching the sky and water falling from the mountains thousands of feet below making thunderous noise. I said to myself, if only the people back home could see this.

Our cabin was located in the valley at the edge of the river that flows throughout. It was quaint, with cots as beds and a small area that could be called a kitchen. The weather was beautiful, approximately 70 degrees with a gentle, cool breeze blowing. Patches of clouds covered the dark-blue sky here. The wind made a swishing noise as it passed through the trees.

After unpacking, I walked to the riverbank sat there basking in the sun watching the clear, cool water as it flowed downward. I closed my eyes and imagined that I was in Fiji. The sounds of the water, the wind, the sun, and the serenity added to the memories of home. Nevertheless, instead of feeling lonely, I felt a sense of peace.

I heard a noise, turned around, and saw Len walking in my direction. He stood next to me, put his hands on his hips, and said, "Beautiful, isn't it? I bet it reminds you of Fiji."

I smiled and replied, "It is gorgeous, and even prettier than anything in Fiji was."

We spent our days hiking to the waterfalls, lying in the sun, and swimming in the cold river. I was eager to swim in the clean, clear water. Finding a deep spot in the river, I dove in. I was in for the shock of my life. The water was painfully cold. I immediately swam to the edge and came out shivering and with a headache.

Now I knew why so many people were basking in the sun and only a handful were daring to go into the water. I quickly dried myself and lay in the sun to get warm. I must have fallen asleep, because when I awoke, the sun was beginning to set. The weather began to get cool, and the wind could be heard howling through the redwood trees. Every night we sat by the warm fire enjoying hot chocolate. The sky was clear and full of stars. In the silence of the night, the sounds of the waterfalls could be heard as water came thundering down the mountains.

Mere words cannot describe the natural wonders Yosemite offers. The breathtaking beauty that nature had endowed on this valley is one of the wonders of the world. While driving, we came to a bend where the traffic had stopped on the narrow road. As the car slowly moved closer to the point where everyone was stopping, I saw a huge tree with the road going right through the trunk.

I could not believe my eyes. First, I had never seen a tree that big, and second, there was a road going right through it! Now I had seen everything. This was the ultimate. Len drove slowly as we approached the tree. A sign said, "Welcome to the Wawona tree, the largest living tree in the world." The car slowly passed through the tree. Warren had stepped out and positioned himself in front and took pictures from different angles.

The history of the Wawona tree and how a road was built right through it was quite interesting. The pioneers and stagecoach owners could not find a flat piece of land around the mountains to take the stagecoach. They had to either go ten miles out of the way or cut the tree. Instead of destroying this beautiful and historical tree, they cut a hole in the massive trunk and built the road directly through it.

Years later, the road was paved and slightly widened for cars to drive through. Again, my mind switched back to Fiji. I wished that the entire family could see this beauty and the American ingenuity. Fiji had its beautiful beaches, rivers, and all the other natural beauties, but this was nature and men working together to keep the splendor and find a practical use for the big tree.

After spending two weeks in Yosemite Valley, it was time to head back home to Glendale. It was rather sad leaving the valley. Looking back as the car began climbing the hill, we could see the waterfalls; the half-dome, the mountain that appeared as if someone or something had cut it in half; and the tall redwood trees that were reaching for the sky.

Camping was much like being back home—cooking outside, showering in cold water, and living outdoors. For the short duration of this outing, I wasn't homesick. Having a good time made me temporarily forget the feeling of loneliness. The surroundings created a mood that was relaxed and carefree. After all, this was the seventh wonder of the world. A place where time had stood still and the natural beauty brought out the best in people. The car climbed higher and higher until the valley looked like a miniature model. The valley disappeared from sight when the car turned a corner and went into the tunnel.

There were still three weeks remaining in the summer vacation. Len's vacation was over, and he had to go back to work. However, since he worked from 4:00 PM to 11:00 PM, we still had time during the day for outings. Glendale had a big community swimming pool directly across the street from the community college. The pool was about three miles from our house. For the remainder of the vacation, we went swimming during the day. I would climb to the top of the diving board and dive into the blue water. At times, I did flips in the air, just to show off.

One day, while getting ready to make my dive from the board, a boy pushed me into the water. He was shouting obscenities at me. I fell into the pool on my stomach, causing me excruciating pain. I swam to the edge of the pool, got out, and stood there wanting to find the boy and beat the hell out of him. Len was lying in the sun, but I did not want to tell him about the incident.

Then, I saw the boy who pushed me walk by with an older boy and a man. The boy pointed at me and said, "That's the black boy I pushed in the water." By now, my physical pain had subsided, but the mental pain of being ridiculed was still persisting. Although I ignored people when they made their foolish remarks or moved away as I swam, I knew that their actions were motivated by prejudice.

Because of the negative experiences, I sometimes did not like going anywhere alone. Actually, Len did not let me go too many places by myself. If I did go to the movies or shopping, I went with Garcie or some other friends. Once, when I could not find Garcie and Len was at work, I decided to go to a matinee by myself to see a cowboy film. Getting to the theater was no big challenge. I had already mastered walking down Brand Boulevard to the shops and theaters.

It was still summer, and many of the students were spending their days at the pool, beach, and movie theaters. While sitting in the theater and enjoying the film, I felt something hit my back. I looked back and could not see what it was or from where it came. A few minutes later, I felt something hit the back of my neck. Turning around, I noticed a few boys laughing. Not knowing if they were the ones throwing things at me, I ignored them.

When the movie was over and the lights came on, I stood up to see if there were some guilty-looking boys. I noticed the four boys who were laughing earlier. They were pointing at me and carrying on a conversation. I looked in their direction and proceeded to walk out of the theater.

I stopped at the concession stand to buy a popsicle to keep me company on my walk home. As I was walking away from the counter, the four boys approached me. They looked like high-school students, but I wasn't certain. One of them walked up to me and said, "Boy, if we see you in this theater again, we're going to kick your ass." I was stunned and dumbfounded.

They laughed and walked away. I remained standing perplexed and angry with myself for not responding. All I wanted to do was beat the hell out of them. However, I was more upset at myself than at them. How could I let these people treat me like this and not do anything? In Fiji, no one treated me like this, and if someone did, I would have knocked the hell out of him.

All the way home, I kept playing the scenario of the boys laughing at me and the one boy with the brownish blond hair telling me what he was going to do to me. What did I do to these people to cause them to display such hatred? I wished that Garcie was with me. Together, we would have taken care of those punks. The more I thought, the angrier I became. I wished I had never come to America. Sure, I had many possessions here that I did not have in Fiji and money to do whatever I wanted. However, being called names and threatened made me feel very low and despondent.

At this juncture, I would have traded the materialistic possessions for friendship and peace of mind. Perhaps things were difficult because in Fiji, I was a big fish in the little pond, and in America, I was just an ordinary little fish that was being knocked around. I missed the comfort of familiar surroundings, friends, and family.

The subtle behaviors exhibited by people made me self-conscious and added to my misery. These negative incidents made me feel sorry for myself and ask myself, "What am I doing in this country?" I wondered what my parents would say and do if they knew about my plight.

At fourteen, I did not have the understanding of what motivated people to behave in such a manner. In addition, I was not conscious of the racist attitude that existed in many parts of the country toward non-whites. At this point in my life, ignorance was bliss. Not knowing the real reason for some people's behaviors actually shielded me from further feelings of humiliation. I knew Len somewhat understood what I was experiencing, but I did not want to burden him with this inescapable problem.

Overall, Glendale was a beautiful and friendly place to live. People were always out talking with each other or doing something around the house. They would wave and say hello when someone walked down the street. This was an all-American city. Doors were rarely locked. One could say that Glendale was the community epitomized by the television show The Adventures of Ozzie and Harriet.

I attempted to cheer myself by thinking about all the positive experiences I had and the nice people I had met. After all, not everyone was bad, just a few ignorant people who didn't know any better.

I have always liked wide-open spaces, the countryside where horses and other animals roam freely. I suppose that's why I was, and still am, a big fan of Western movies. Len knew I liked horses, so he took me to an area in Glendale and in Burbank where they had horse stables. Being in this area was like being in a cowboy movie. People were riding horses on trails, all dressed in Western outfits. I could not believe that we were only a few miles from our house. Len asked, "Do you want to learn how to ride horses?" I smiled and nodded my head. He spoke to one of the men, who looked like he had just stepped out of a John Wayne movie, and asked him about the feasibility of lessons. The man informed Len that the ideal time to receive lessons was on Saturdays.

Len made arrangements for one of his nieces, Jo Ann, and I to begin taking riding lessons the following Saturday. Just the thought of getting on a horse and riding through the hills of Griffith Park made me shiver.

It was Saturday, and it was a beautiful day. I woke up early filled with anticipation for the horseback-riding lesson. Our lesson was scheduled for nine o'clock, but I was ready by seven. I could hardly wait to get to the Pickwick Stables. As soon as the car pulled into the parking lot, Jo Ann and I jumped out and headed for the stable. When our turn came for the lesson, the trainer spoke to us about the do's and don'ts of getting on and off a horse, and how to treat the horse. The trainer's name was Mr. King. He looked like a real cowboy with blue jeans, brown leather boots, a plaid shirt, and brown cowboy hat.

Mr. King was very patient with all the riders. He stood in the middle of the ring and watched each one of us as we made our initial rounds with the horses. I was holding the reins too tightly, and he walked over, adjusted the reins, and showed me exactly how to hold the reins to guide the horse. He was a real teacher who smiled as he taught us. When my horse began to trot a little, I began bouncing up and down without control. Mr. King stopped my horse and showed me how to post. He explained that I should use my knees to go up and down with the horse and not bounce around. He was right because my whole body was beginning to hurt from the bouncing.

The riding lesson was over within an hour, although it seemed as if we were on the horses all day. My back and legs were very sore. I never knew that riding a horse was such a painful experience. Nevertheless, Jo Ann and I had a lot of fun. As we came out of the gate, Len was there to greet us with his usual smile and wave. "You really looked good on the horses," he commented. "Are you hungry? Let's go to the International House of Pancakes for breakfast."

Before we left, I ran back to the stable, thanked Mr. King for the lesson, and said, "I can't wait until next Saturday."

What a great weekend we had horseback riding, swimming, and then going out to dinner on Saturday night. To top it off, Len took us to Knotts Berry Farm on Sunday. This amusement park had train and stagecoach rides, a merry-go-round, water rides, and many other mechanical rides. I really enjoyed the Ferris wheel ride. This was the biggest Ferris wheel ride I had ever seen. It took you very high up and came down fast, making you feel as though you were going to lose your stomach.

Knotts was modeled after a town in the Western days. There were also many eating places throughout the park made to look like old-time saloons or cafes. People could also pan for gold, witness a train robbery, shoot at various shooting galleries, and try to win prizes from numerous games.

During dinner at one of the eateries at Knotts, Len leaned over to me and asked, "Are you having fun?"

I smiled and said, "Yes, thank you for bringing us."

Warren also said, "Yeah, thanks, Unkie, we are having a lot of fun."

Throughout Glendale, Len was known as Unkie, short for Uncle Len. He was an uncle to everyone, children and adults alike. Len was the father figure to all the children in the neighborhood. He also helped the adults when they came to him for some kind of assistance. A day didn't go by when some kid didn't come running down the driveway yelling, "Unkie, take me to the park or to get something to eat."

If he could not take them, he reached into his pocket and gave them some money so they could buy a burger or an ice cream. No matter where we went, Len always took a car full of youngsters. He received enjoyment from watching others having fun. He believed that there was no reason for people to be unhappy, especially children, and that people should help one another.

I was young and naïve and did not know what a great man Len truly was. It would be a few years before I would find out all about Len as a scholar and human being. The fact that he brought me, a total stranger, to raise and educate was a great feat in itself. Nevertheless, his humanism was expansive and immeasurable. He worked all week, but never said he was too tired to take us places.

We walked around the park and enjoyed the old Western town. I was mesmerized by the chicken that played the piano. People would put some money in a slot, a green light would go on, and the chicken that was in a glass cage would run and start playing a miniature piano. The chicken stopped when the green light went off. Some food came down a small tube into a dish for the chicken as a reward.

I was in awe. I knew that America was a great place, but a chicken playing the piano was the ultimate. Not only were the people smart in this country, but so were the animals. It was getting so that almost nothing was a surprise anymore.

The glorious days of summer were quickly coming to an end. I could think and reflect on all the great times we had at Yosemite, the amusement parks, and of course the visits to the mountains and beaches. Len and I were sitting on the porch one evening on a Sunday, and he asked, "Well, did you enjoy your summer?"

I replied, "I had a great time."

He gave me his usual smile and said, "Are you ready for school?"

I confessed that I wished the summer had been a little longer and that I was not looking forward to going back to school.

The beginning of school was only a few days away, and my apprehension was already high. Nevertheless, one thing was certain: I would not be alone, because Garcie was there, and we had made a few friends.

Our conversation on the porch was more than a discussion about school or the summer; it was also about my life in America. Len stated, "I have been worried about you being homesick. I have heard you crying on several occasions."

I looked at him and told him, "Don't worry; I am really enjoying my life."

"Would you like to go back to Fiji?" he asked.

I was shocked at the question and quickly replied, "No."

My response was without hesitation. After all, Len brought me to the United States and was raising me as his own son. No way could I let him down by telling him that I was still homesick. I could not be ungrateful and say that I still missed home after such a fun-filled summer. Len spared no expenses to make sure that all of us had a wonderful time. However, deep inside I longed for my friends, playing soccer, and of course going fishing. Len went inside and made himself a martini.

The evening was beautiful, a cool breeze was blowing, and the sun was slowly disappearing behind the hills of Glendale. I asked Len where he went to school. He shared his experience about growing up in New Zealand until he was twelve years old and then moving to England. "My father was a minister with the Church of England, and he was sent to New Zealand before I was born," Len said. "New Zealand was beautiful. We lived in Christchurch, the South Island, which was less developed than the North Island, where Auckland is located. I liked playing in the open fields and going to school in the small country schoolhouse.

"Since my father was a minister, my brother, two sisters, and I had to be very active in the church. I liked the church in the beginning, but began to wonder about the purpose of religion when I was thirteen years old. That's when we moved to England."

"Did you like England?" I inquired.

"Well, we were in London, a big and crowded city. I didn't really care for the crowd and all the crap," Len replied.

"So, you went to junior high in England?"

"Yup! It was a snooty school called Harrow. This is where all the high-brow, spoiled rich kids went."

We spoke for over an hour. I was really interested in Len's schooling and how he became the champion of the poor and the working class. During our first conversation and many that followed, I learned that Len was always against the so-called "feudal class" of England and wanted to be a member of the working class. He came from an aristocratic family from his grandmother's side. It was his grandmother who helped him get into Harrow. Len entered Harrow when he was fourteen, around the time the First World War started. However, before he could get into Harrow, he had to attend a prep school to polish his language skills. The kids at the prep school made fun of him and called him names because of his New Zealand accent. "I found myself as an outsider, an inferior person," Len said.

All through Harrow, Len read the classics such as Dickens. "I hated sports, so I buried myself in the books. That's how I was able to get a scholarship to Oxford. However, before going to Oxford, I spent a year in the army. The war, the bourgeoisie, and the Oxford scene were getting boring. I wanted to do something about the plight of the poor people to make their lives better. So, when I was twenty-one years old, I left Oxford and England and came to America. Life wasn't easy. I struggled, until I joined the labor movement and eventually helped John L. Lewis with the Congress of Industrial Workers (CIO)."

# Chapter Eleven:  Back to School

I was looking forward to the opening of school, but at the same time, I was apprehensive. I dreaded the idea of having to endure the insults from a number of the students and being treated rather harshly by some of the teachers. However, I was having too much fun to worry about things that had not yet happened.

The exhilarating days and nights of the summer had temporarily made me forget about my loneliness. After all, the weekends were going to be filled with short trips to exciting places. We were still taking riding lessons on Saturdays. I was really beginning to control the horse and not bounce up and down quite so much. Mr. King, the riding teacher, was very complimentary of my progress and said that I could go out on the trail soon. Oh yeah, me riding like the cowboys in the movies out on the open trail!

It was the first day of the new school year. Students were walking from all directions toward the school. Len pulled the car in front of the school, and Warren and I jumped out. We were the upperclassmen, the big ninth graders. It appeared as if everyone in Glendale was going to school. Hundreds of students were walking through the door talking loudly and yelling hello to the friends they had not seen all summer.

I immediately began looking for Garcie. Warren saw a few of his friends, said, "See you later," and walked away with them. I entered the school and headed for my homeroom class. Homeroom was the place we received our program card showing our classes. The first day was always hectic—students running around looking for their rooms and some inquiring about changing their programs or teachers.

The first person I saw in homeroom was Garcie. I sat in the chair next to him. "Hey, how are you? I am so glad to see you in here," I said.

Garcie smiled and said, "I was looking for you in the morning and was a little worried when I didn't see you."

"Yeah, we were running a little late this morning."

After we received our programs, we found that we only had physical education together. Our anticipation of having some of the same classes was extinguished. At least we were in the same homeroom and gym class. The homeroom teacher was very nice. He explained all the rules and regulations of the school, asked us about the accuracy of our programs, and informed us that we could see him if we had any problems. As soon as the bell rang, everyone dashed out of the class and into the crowded hallway. I yelled at Garcie, "See you at nutrition by the eating area." Then I was off to finding the first-period class.

Walking down the hall and looking for the room number, I felt someone push me. I turned around, and a boy just yelled, "Move out of the way, nigger." I told him that I was not in his way and that there was plenty of room for him to walk by me. He stood there balling his fist as if to fight. Just then, I saw the room number and walked into my science class.

I guess this boy had a problem of some kind and wanted to pick on someone; in this case, it happened to be me. I was angry about being called a "nigger." Someone else had called me that before, and I asked Len what it meant. At first, Len was very upset that I was called that name, then he gave me the definition and explained to me why some people used that term. He told me that it was a very nasty word that people used toward dark people to put them down.

The rest of the school day was pretty hectic, but it was exciting seeing some of the students who had become my friends. In due time, one day led into another. I was beginning to enjoy school. The classes were difficult, but if I studied diligently and did all my homework, I was able to keep up. Of course, I still had problems processing the language. Sometimes, instead of saying that I didn't understand what was being said, I smiled and nodded as if I understood. Actually, this was not the best thing to do, especially in my algebra class. I pretended that I understood because I didn't want to look stupid. As a result, I received a D in the class. The teacher gave me the D because she liked me and felt sorry for me. In reality, I failed the class. I did repeat the class later and received a C.

It was very frustrating not being able to understand some of the conversations. Many times when people were talking and looking at me, I thought they were talking about me. When one doesn't understand what is being said, and people look at him and laugh, he has a tendency to become paranoid.

Although school was becoming easier, facing my loneliness was not getting any better. Sometimes when I came home from school and nobody was there, I would feel an inexplicable feeling pass through me. I didn't know what this feeling was, but I knew that it was related to my loneliness. These were the times when my homesickness was most pronounced. I missed sitting in front of the house by the big mango tree and speaking with my friends or listening to one of the elders telling stories.

Storytelling was a favorite pastime for the older folks. Occasionally, they told us ghost stories and during other times tales about certain unexplained events that occurred in the Islands. There was the story about the turtle that saved a boy who was drowning and brought him all the way back to the village and one about the floating island that went from place to place spreading its beauty. Sometimes we stayed up half the night listening to stories.

People gathered every evening to socialize and catch up with the events of the day. The radio station was operational only a few hours a day, so receiving the news was difficult. Besides, only a handful of the people had radios. Homes of people who did have a radio became the gathering places. There never was a shortage of human interaction.

Whenever I thought of the family and hanging out, my homesickness increased. It was very evident that in America people did not get together very much. After work or school, people went home, watched television, and mainly stayed inside for the evening. In Fiji, everyone was out in the streets talking or visiting.

If I wasn't with Garcie or at the library, I usually found myself alone. Since Len left home at three for work, there wasn't anybody at the house by the time I came home from school. The other kids usually went out with their friends or were busy doing their own thing. Warren was involved in numerous school activities that kept him there late.

Most of the time, I would turn on the television and watch cartoons. Besides liking cartoons, I discovered that I learned English by watching the cartoons. In cartoons when they spoke a word, they followed it with an action. I quickly learned to associate the actions with the spoken word. Later in life when I became a teacher, I used the same technique to teach students who understood little or no English.

I wished some of my teachers in Glendale were as sensitive to my needs. They simply gave us the books, explained the subject on the board, and asked us to complete the assignment while they sat at their desks. I experienced most of the difficulties in English and other academic classes that required comprehension and interpretation of the material presented. My oral language was improving rapidly, although I still had an accent.

Some of my classmates made fun of me when I spoke in class. One time, even the teacher stopped me in the middle of the sentence and said, "I can't understand what you are saying, so just ask one of the students later." Her comment only made me withdraw further and refrain from asking any questions.

The insensitive social studies teacher was not quite as demeaning, but he attempted to embarrass me by saying that I needed to be able to stand in front of the class and name every state and their capitals, and spell them. He knew that this was a nearly impossible task for someone like me who was just learning the language. However, I could not be humiliated twice in one day. Therefore, I studied day and night and all weekend memorizing and practicing. Since I am an auditory learner, I made songs and recited the states and the capitals aloud.

All weekend, Len assumed the role of my audience and tutor, helping me prepare for the big challenge. On Monday, I stood in front of the class, named all the fifty states and their capitals, and spelled them correctly. The teacher and the entire class were in awe of my performance. Some of the students applauded as I made my way back to my seat, but the teacher did not utter a word.

In my school back home, I did not have to face such problems. In fact, the teachers usually asked me to explain and help other students. Now, instead of being the top dog, I was the subject of ridicule. During these trying times, I wished I had never come to this country.

Len's daughter, Shirley, and her husband, Gordon, would drop by to visit, or we went to their house in Pomona. Going to their house was an adventure because we drove through many cities and on various freeways. Pomona was out in the country, about thirty-five miles from Glendale. There was something romantic about the Sunday drives. It seemed that every family in America got in their cars and went somewhere on Sundays. You could see cars filled with families driving in every direction.

I liked the place where Shirley and Gordon lived because it had rolling hills and wide-open spaces. Gordon usually made barbeque chicken and steaks with corn and potatoes. I had never tasted barbeque before I came to America. I really loved the chicken and corn. It was always a great treat to sink my teeth into a drumstick or breast of chicken. I remember one time we were visiting, and Gordon asked me if I wanted to ride a motorcycle. Never having been on a motorcycle, I was afraid. Gordon said, "Try to get on the small one, and I will show you what to do." I saw a young boy coming on a small motorcycle. Gordon said, "Look at him on the minibike; it ain't so hard." I was tempted but decided against the ride. So, Gordon gave me a ride on his bike, while I held on to him fearing for my life as he gunned the bike and took off.

Gordon was a great guy. He was about twenty-three years old and worked as a mechanic. He loved working on cars. There wasn't anything he didn't know about engines. He spoke softly with a Texas accent and always had a smile. All the people in the neighborhood liked Gordon. He was always fixing cars or the young people's minibikes. He offered to get a minibike for me, but Len said it was too dangerous. Although I liked the bikes, I was glad Len said no, because I was afraid to ride one.

Shirley, my American sister, was low key and mellow. She was very curious about Fiji and the other South Pacific Islands. When we were at her house, she played some Tahitian music that she had found in a record store. She said, "I figured this music would make you feel at home." She confided in me that her dad was truly happy to have me. She said that when he came back from Fiji, he constantly talked about my family and me. She even leaned over to me during dinner and whispered, "I am happy to have a brother."

Len and his wife, Caroline, adopted Shirley when she was a baby. She did not know her biological parents or if she had any siblings. She loved Len, and he adored her, although he was a little disappointed that she got married right after high school. Shirley said that her mom and dad were very upset at her for getting married so young, but did not stay angry for long. She said, "My dad loves Gordon. You know, Gordon is so nice, quiet, and will do anything my dad asks. He has a lot of respect for my dad; he won't even smoke in front of him."

We had numerous weekend visitations to Pomona, including going to the Los Angeles County Fair that is held in Pomona. We also took trips to the San Bernardino Mountains and Big Bear Lake. It was in the San Bernardino Mountains that I saw snow for the first time. I had seen snow in films, but never had any real idea about its texture or why it was cold.

While we were visiting the mountains one day, the weather became cloudy and dark. In Fiji the weather turned that way before a heavy rainfall. So I turned to Len and said, "Looks like it's going to rain."

He said, "Maybe, or it may snow, because it is cold, too cold for rain." Len asked Warren and me if we wanted hot chocolate. We both jumped at the idea and began looking for a place to buy our hot chocolate. When we came out with our hot chocolates, we were surprised to see the ground turning white and tiny white flakes falling from the sky.

All I knew about snow was what I had seen in the films. To actually feel the white flakes falling from the sky was extraordinary. As I stood out attempting to catch the flakes, I began to shiver. My hands were getting numb. I had never experienced such a feeling. The trees, the roofs of buildings, and the ground were all draped in the white rain called snow. Oh, what a beautiful sight. Watching the flakes fall to the ground and the landscape changing made me forget about the coldness. This wasn't rain, but the roads were becoming wet as were my clothes and hair. Suddenly, the chill pierced through my skin, and I could feel the chill in my bones.

We quickly jumped into the warm car to escape from the blistering wind and cold. "Turn the heater to high," Warren yelled. "It's freezing in here." We both were shivering.

Len laughed. "Look at you two; first you insisted on playing in the cold snow and now you can't get out of it fast enough."

"I love the snow," I replied, "but I didn't know that this thing called snow can be so cold. In the films, people run around, throw the stuff at each other, and do not seem to shiver."

Laughing at my naïveté, Len gave me a brief lesson about reality and the world of movies. He let me know that what we were seeing and experiencing was real and what we see in films was make believe. I thought to myself, boy do I have a lot to learn.

Learning came in various forms. It was difficult to comprehend some of the nuances and traditional sayings. Nevertheless, I pretended to understand whatever was happening. Educators assume so much about the way we learn. Not all children learn the same way, and above all, not all children have the same frame of reference. I remember the English teacher asking me to describe the similarities between wood and coal. I looked at her, dumbfounded because I did not know anything about coal. I knew that wood was used to make furniture, build houses, and for fire. In Fiji, we used wood to cook our food. I had never heard of coal. She assumed that I knew about coal. In fact, I had only recently learned about snow, and that alone was quite an experience.

# Chapter Twelve:
# Learning More About Race and Sensitivity

We always remember incidences in our lives that leave lasting impressions and have a great impact on us. I remember one night in 1963 when two of my friends, Art and Deter, and I had gone to see a movie, *Bye Bye Birdie*, an obscure film. Nevertheless, I will forever remember this movie.

We came out of the theater at approximately 8:30 PM. It was a rather cool and dark evening. Walking home, we joked and laughed to pass the time. Art and Deter lived close to each other, and I had to walk a half a mile further to reach home. After saying goodbye to my friends, I turned the corner from Brand Boulevard to Windsor Road. I proceeded to walk at a rapid pace.

Suddenly, I noticed a red flashing light coming toward me. It was a police car. It pulled directly in front of me, and two police officers got out of the car and yelled, "Get up against the wall." I put my hands up and against the wall. They told me to spread my legs. One officer asked, "Boy, what are you doing here at this time of the night?" I was terrified and could not give an answer. This was my first encounter with the law. Bizarre thoughts about what was going to happen to me ran through my mind. Was I going to be taken to jail and then sent back to Fiji? He shined his big black flashlight in my face and again repeated, "What are you doing here? Let me see some identification."

I was so afraid that I was shaking. The policemen were wearing guns. Were they going to shoot me if I said something wrong? They looked angry. In my broken English and quivering voice, I attempted to explain to them that I was going home and that it was only a few blocks away. One of the policemen responded, "Don't lie. Turn around and show me your identification." I reached into my pocket and pulled out the school identification. Both of the officers shined the flashlight on the card and said something to each other.

Finally, one officer said, "You are that new kid from some island somewhere who came here to go to school." I explained that we had gone to see a movie, and my friends had gone home. They discussed something amongst themselves and asked me to sit in the back of the car. I was so afraid that I could not even walk. Oh no, I thought, these policemen were going to take me to jail.

I cautiously moved toward the car. One officer opened the door and asked me to sit down. When they both sat down, they asked me for my address. I was surprised at their inquiry. They began asking me questions about Fiji and how I happened to come to America. The officer driving the car stated that he had read something about me in the *Glendale News Press*.

The tone of their voices and mannerisms toward me became very pleasant. I felt a sense of relief in knowing that they knew who I was and were taking me home. The police car pulled closed to the curb in front of our driveway, and the officers told me to be careful and to not walk alone at night. I thanked them for the ride, waved good night, and ran into the house.

Now I really knew that I was a stranger in a strange land. Having been stopped and almost taken to jail because of my appearance was horrifying. Just when I was beginning to become accustomed to this new way of life, I was reminded that I did not belong in the community.

My two friends didn't care about my skin color or my accent. They looked at me as one of their classmates and hung around with me. But the law of the city and the prevailing attitudes of the citizens were different. If you were not white, you could not be in the city after sunset. What if I didn't have my school identification card? Would the police have really taken me to jail, or would they have taken me in their car and dropped me off at the border of Los Angeles and Glendale?

I did not tell Len about my ordeal with the police. He already felt bad about my having to endure the hardships. Furthermore, he already knew about the horrors of being a dark-skinned person in a white city.

After all, this was 1963, and the Civil Rights Bill was not passed until 1964. Individual states and cities could treat their citizens any way they wanted. There were no federal laws that specifically forbade cities and states from discriminating against individuals based on their race, ethnicity, and color. The land of milk and honey was great if one looked as white as milk and not brown like honey.

The fact that I was from an island did have its advantages. People were a little kinder when they learned that I was from a remote island in the South Pacific Ocean. Surfing was becoming popular, and of course, Hawaii was the focus of attention. The teenagers wanted to know all about my surfing experiences in the Islands. I was rapidly becoming a popular person in school and in the city, especially when I wore my island shirts to school. Surfer dudes wanted to hang out with me and go surfing on weekends. Realistically, I had never surfed in Fiji, but I did learn to surf while visiting Hawaii. It was nice to be popular again, albeit in a small circle.

A few of the kids even invited me to their homes for dinner. At first, the parents looked at me strangely, but once they realized that I was the "island boy," their attitudes changed somewhat. My loneliness and thoughts about home were less intrusive in my newfound excitement. I was back to my old self. There were times when lying on the beach or on the surfboard waiting for a wave, I thought I was back home. Yes, America was not such a bad place after all.

My English was getting better. The foods that previously smelled and tasted awful didn't seem so bad. I was enjoying school, and the sadness and tears that used to be my companions had all but disappeared. I was not afraid to ask questions in the classroom and began to participate in after-school activities.

Yes, there still were incidences where students called me names or adults gave me looks filled with disdain, but these were miniscule compared to what I experienced during my first year. I worked diligently to lose my accent and read whatever I could to improve my reading and comprehension.

Then came a day when all my abilities to communicate in English were put to the test. In English class, we were asked to read a book and be prepared to make a book report. I had read the book *Of Mice and Men* by John Steinbeck and written a book report. The teacher asked me to stand in front of the class and give an oral report. I felt confident about giving the oral report. Having read the book twice and memorizing the dialogue between two of the main characters, George and Lenny, I knew I would be a hit.

However, much to my chagrin, soon after I began, the teacher looked at me and said, "Go and sit down until you learn to speak better, and I can understand what you are saying." I was mortified. Some of the students laughed at the teacher's statement while I stood there in disbelief. For an instant, I could not move. My entire body felt numb.

Without a word, I slowly walked back to my desk. I could not believe what had just happened. The teacher had indeed made fun of me and showed no sensitivity. I felt a lump in my throat. I was crying inside, wanting to run away, hide, or disappear. It wasn't my fault that I had an accent. I knew the material, the main theme, and characters. What if my accent was a little thick? That was no reason to humiliate me.

As I sat with the lump in my throat and tears welling in my eyes, I thought to myself, I wish I were your boss. I would fire you right now. How could she be so insensitive? Even if she was prejudiced, she was still a teacher and should have encouraged me instead of disgracing me. I felt bitterness and anger. Here I was, attempting to impress her and my classmates, and I got shot down without the opportunity to express myself.

Not every experience was negative, and not all teachers were insensitive. Some teachers were considerate and permitted me extra time to finish projects and reports. The science teacher even assigned a bright student to be a buddy and help me with my science project.

David Fujikawa was an American of Japanese descent. He grew up in Glendale. Although he knew some of the people were prejudiced because of his race, he considered himself an American. David was sensitive about the fact that the other students would make fun of us if we made even the slightest mistake. He always took the utmost care to insure that our work was the best. In reality, it was his work since he did most of the writing. I appreciated David's assistance and his friendship. He never made rude comments or tried to demean me in front of his friends or the teacher. Thanks to David Fujikawa, I passed science.

# Chapter Thirteen: Still the Darkness

It is difficult to explain, but no matter how much fun I was having, there was always a feeling of emptiness that haunted me. I could not shake the strange fear that was constantly interfering with my every thought. Sometimes I didn't even want to go outside or interact with anyone. Perhaps it was all in my mind.

One thought that did occupy my mind was that of home. I wondered if the family missed me as much as I missed them. Did they even think about me? After all, they all had each other. I didn't even have anyone to speak the language with. I would have even settled for a good old home-cooked hot and spicy meal.

When I think back to those days, my eyes still become watery. Language and culture are the strongest bonds human beings have outside of the family relationship. That's why it is so difficult for some of the students to adjust to the socialization process in schools and society. They live in households whose cultural values and customs are totally different from the ones they are taught in schools and see out in the mainstream society. Vast majorities of the youngsters have problems coping with the dual cultural existence. Some rebel against their parents while others drop out of both societies and seek solace through drugs and alcohol.

First-generation immigrants always have tough choices. They migrate to seek a better life, yet miss their homeland. No matter how hard they try to assimilate into the new culture, they still face insurmountable obstacles. They cannot go back to their homelands because in most cases they sell everything to migrate.

Another reason they cannot go back is because they would be considered failures in their country if they were to return. People also remain because they want their children to receive good education and improve their economic stature. Therefore, numerous social and, in some cases, cultural sacrifices are made by the immigrants.

My parents made the decision for me to migrate. I, however, wanted to go back and enjoy the simple life of the Islands, spending my days fishing, swimming, and hanging out instead of sitting in front of the television vegetating. In the beginning, I was totally enamored with the modern society and the materialistic conveniences available at every turn. As time passed, I became like everyone else and took everything for granted. The newness had passed, and the daily routine became nothing but mundane.

I had turned fifteen, and life was becoming more complicated. The teenage code of conduct was tough. We all had to behave in certain ways, listen to certain types of music, and dress in certain styles. Nevertheless, I followed the styles and wished with every breath that I could escape from this harsh reality. My desire was to go back to a place where family life, togetherness, and caring for one another dominated the culture. I did not want to be judged by the style of clothes I wore and the number of materialistic goods in my possession.

Len was extremely sensitive to my needs and rarely interfered. He wanted me to receive the best possible education and stay away from anything or anybody who would lead me in the wrong direction. We usually talked about my social life and the difficulties I encountered. One day during our usual conversation on the porch, he asked me if I would like to go back to Fiji for a visit. I jumped at the idea and quickly replied, "Yes, I would love to go back."

He confided in me that he had seen me crying and felt bad about my position. He said, "I knew you would miss your family when you came, but I had misjudged as to how much."

I let him know that I was truly appreciative of his love for me and the kindness he had shown me. "You know you are my father, mother, brother, and the entire family. What more could I ask for? You have been wonderful to me." I walked over, gave him a big hug, and said, "I love you."

That night, I could not sleep. Summer vacation was three months away. These were going to be the longest three months of my life. I was going back home, to the familiar surroundings, to the family, and above all, to a place where the language, food, and cultural activities were a part of me. My mind wandered in all directions, and my mouth began to water at the thought of all the fresh, tasty, home-cooked goodies. In America, I had everything, but the one component of my life that was not fulfilled was that of being together with family and friends.

Since I was a little boy, I dreamt about faraway places and what it would be like to live somewhere other than Fiji. I used to read books and magazines about the adventures of Sinbad, the journeys of Captain Cook, and all the other explorers. I would lose myself in these books and imagine that I was one of these adventurers. The movies I would see added to my desire for travel. American and British movies showed big buildings, fast cars, and people dressed in fancy clothes. I would close my eyes and try to visualize how it would feel to be one of those people.

Never in my wildest imagination did I think that someday my dreams would come to fruition. Now that I was in a faraway land, all I wished for was to go back home. The saying "The grass always seems greener on the other side" is positively a statement that described my state of mind. Here I was, living a luxurious life that I had always wished for, and yet I longed for the life I had left. The family was envious of the life I was living in America with all its modern trappings. In actuality, I was envious of them. At this time in my life, the modern comforts did not seem as important. Perhaps it's better to dream and wish than to have the dreams come true.

My excitement of going back added to my loneliness. The same question always ran through my mind. "Why was I here?" This question was rhetorical since I knew I was sent to receive an education. Regardless of the reason I left Fiji, I could not believe that my parents would give me up and let me spend my life in loneliness. I was missing the most critical aspect of growing up on an island. Instead of "hanging loose," I was constantly rushing around from school to library to home. At home, my constant companion was the television.

I am not totally critical of the television, because I learned the language and a lot about the world from watching the so-called "boob tube." Television is a great babysitter. After finishing my homework, I dove into the world of television. What better way to pass time than to stare mindlessly at a screen that required no thinking? Weekdays were rough because Garcie was not permitted to go anywhere unless it was with his family, and Len was working. We spoke on the telephone, but that was not the same as hanging out.

Despite the loneliness and occasional racial problems at school, I made every attempt to succeed academically. I did not want to disgrace the family and make Len think that he had made a mistake. Len pretty much left me alone to choose my friends. However, he was cautious about where we went and the character of my friends. He constantly spoke to me about knowing right from wrong and the dangers of alcohol and drugs. I knew about alcohol, but had never heard of drugs.

We did see boys and girls smoking in certain corners of the school during the breaks, but these groups hung around together and rarely associated with others on campus. I never had problems with any of these individuals. In fact, some of the boys were very friendly with me. At times when others were harassing me, the so-called "bad boys" came to my assistance.

I didn't make snap judgments about people because of the way they dressed or behaved. I always smiled and said hello to everyone. Even today, I try not to make assumptions about any individual's character or personality, until he or she portrays some kind of behavior that warrants a judgment.

The classes at school remained challenging, but not like they were in the beginning. My comprehension of the English language and ability to communicate orally and in writing had improved. I didn't worry about graduating from junior high school. However, Len did have some concerns about my ability to perform in school while trying to acclimate to the American way of life.

As June approached, I could not wait to get out of school and board the plane. Graduation was only a few weeks away. Len had already bought a roundtrip ticket for me. I was to leave two days after graduation. The last few weeks seemed like an eternity. The days were long, and the weeks seemed like months. I was so excited about the summer vacation that I temporarily lost sight of the final exams.

# Chapter Fourteen: Returning Home

I did not inform anyone back home that I was coming back for a visit. I wanted to surprise everyone. Imagine a member of the family opening the door and finding me standing on the porch or a taxi pulling in front of the house and me stepping out. I bought clothes and souvenirs to take back with me. After all, everyone would want something from the "Great United States."

It was a year and a half ago that I had boarded a plane to come to America. I will never forget February 11, 1962. The day I left the little village on a little island and came to the big city in the big country. I was afraid, sick, and clueless about what was awaiting me. Not even fourteen years old, and I was leaving behind a large, close-knit family to go to a life of modern comforts, but lacking in social relationships. It was the first time I had worn a pair of long pants and put on shoes. On the day of my departure, it was raining, and the weather was uncharacteristically cool.

These days, I had no problem wearing long pants and shoes. I had become an "American Kid." I even spoke English with an American accent. A strange sensation went through me when I boarded the plane. I cannot describe the feeling, but it was a combination of fear and excitement. I was thrilled about going home, but afraid of something. Perhaps I was sad about leaving Len or apprehensive about how I would be accepted by the folks back home. I was not the same boy that left home eighteen months ago.

In the midst of my thoughts, I heard the sound of the screeching tires of the airplane. We had landed in Nadi. Stepping out of the plane, I could feel the humidity and the gentle trade winds blowing. Finally, I was home. That familiar smell was in the air, coconut and mango trees all around. I stood outside for a while and looked around, taking deep breaths of the fresh morning air. Then I quickly walked to the baggage claim area to make sure someone else did not pick up my bags by mistake and take all the gifts.

In the terminal, I heard the people speak, but could not understand what they were saying. The faces looked strange, and the language was foreign. Then I heard someone say, "He probably forgot how to speak the language or is showing off." It occurred to me that because I had not heard either Fijian or Hindi spoken for eighteen months, my ears were not attuned to the languages. Someone asked me if I wanted a taxi, and I could not formulate the words to answer. Had I really forgotten the language, or was I experiencing a temporary lapse? This was déjà vu. I had the same experience when I first went to the United States.

Suddenly, I heard a person asking me where I was going, and I responded, "Samabula." I understood what he was asking and was able to respond. He was a taxi driver.

"Where in Samabula?" he inquired. "What is your father's name?" I gave him my father's and older brother's names. "I know your father. I am from Samabula and recently moved to Nadi. Your family recently moved to Nasinu, four miles." I knew that, but initially the only thing I could blurt out was Samabula.

"How much would you charge for the ride?" I asked. Nasinu was approximately 150 miles away. He said he had another passenger, and we could split the cost. He asked me not to discuss the fare with other person because the amount he was charging me was different from that of the tourist from New Zealand. I was receiving the local rate, and since he knew the family, he could not "rob" me, or he would have to face my father.

Getting into the taxi, I realized that there was a distinct difference in how things were and how I remembered them. The taxi was dirty, the roads were narrow, and the looks on people's faces were that of despair. Had the conditions in Fiji changed so drastically, or was I looking at the island from a different perspective? The car moved noisily along the winding, dusty gravel road. I was lost in the world of scenery. Each tree, beach area, and the thick lush forest reminded me that I was not dreaming.

Abruptly, a loud noise and hissing sound broke my concentration. The driver quickly pulled over to the side of the road. The other passenger was a bit afraid, but I knew that all-too-common sound of a flat tire. Most people drove on these gravel roads with practically bald tires. Getting a flat tire on long journeys was the norm. All cars carried patches to repair the tube and pumps to inflate the tires. This was the first puncture; before the journey was over, we would have at least three more. To compound the problem, the car overheated at one point along the mountainous road.

I knew the ride was going to be long, but the other passenger was not prepared for the adventurous journey along the Fiji roads. I explained to him that his hotel was not as far as where I was going and that he would arrive before sunset. Both of us were upset at the driver for not maintaining the taxi. I informed the driver that the other passenger was upset and I was getting impatient. It was his duty to check the tires and make sure that the radiator had enough water before making such a long journey.

Nevertheless, I passed my time by looking at the scenery and re-embracing the beauty that I had left behind. With nightfall, the ride became endless. I felt sorry for the driver, but was angry with him for spoiling my surprise. Instead of arriving in Nasinu at seven o'clock, we reached our destination at approximately two in the morning. I was tired and exasperated.

The car stopped in front of a house that I did not recognize because of the darkness. This must be the new house because when I departed for the United States we lived in a little shack. The driver turned to me and said, "This is the house. Your father just finished building this house." I jumped out and ran to the front door. My banging brought someone to the door, but instead of saying something, the person ran to the back to get a small pot and bring it to the door. It was my brother Gyan, whom we called by his nickname, Babu. He thought it was five in the morning and the milkman was knocking because they had forgotten to leave the pot for the milk on the porch.

I yelled, "Hey, Babu, why are you running away?"

He stopped in his tracks and hollered, "It's Munna; he is home."

Someone came out with a flashlight. It was Gautam. He immediately grabbed and picked me off the floor. One by one, the rest of the family members began running into the living room from the three bedrooms. I heard my father telling someone to light the benzene light, Coleman lantern. Tears of joy were flowing from my mother's eyes. "Why didn't you tell us you were coming?" bhai asked. For a moment, there was jubilance and disbelief.

The taxi driver appeared at the door with my bags. Bhai recognized him and asked him to stay for tea. I told bhai that I was lucky to have found this driver. I would not have known where to stop because of the darkness. When I left, we had a small tin house, and now in its place stood a three-bedroom house with inside plumbing and water. Bhai told my mother to go and make some tea because he knew the driver and I were exhausted from the long journey.

Everyone sat in the living room opening the bags and trying on the clothes that I had brought. The curiosity about America generated an insurmountable number of questions. I shared my experiences, the positive ones, and gave details about the "land of milk and honey." Bhai asked, "Are you happy in America?"

I gazed at him for a while then scanned the room. Everyone was waiting for my reply. I quietly replied, "Yes."

Bhai said that he knew I was coming. He said that he saw a plane flying in the morning and told my uncle, "Munna is coming home." Bhai was usually right about his intuitions. He had a sixth sense about certain things.

Before we knew it, the sun was appearing in the sky. We had been talking since two, and now it was six o'clock. Not a soul wanted to go to school or work. Bhai told them to let me eat and get some rest. "We can resume our conversations later this afternoon."

The first question out of Gautam's mouth was, "Do you really have your own room with a radio and television?" The others sat there with inquisitive looks on their faces waiting for their turn to ask a question.

One of my cousins asked, "Are the roads as wide as we see in films, and are the cars really fast?" Almost all the inquiries were about materialistic possessions.

Needless to say, I did not get any rest that day. Word quickly spread throughout the community that I was home. People began arriving at our door around eight in the morning and did not stop until ten that night. Almost all the visitors brought something to eat. They all wanted to hear about America. What kind of food did people eat? Was the place really like what they saw in the movies? I told them stories about the freeways, tall buildings, television, and the overabundance of cars in the country. I could see that my family and friends were envisioning life in America vicariously. Gyan mumbled, "I wish I could go to America."

I must have slept for sixteen hours that day. The stream of people flowing in and out of our house had somewhat lessened. That evening, I was treated to a wonderful crab, shrimp, and chicken curry dinner. It was simply delightful to taste that sweet crabmeat cooked spicy hot and the shrimp cooked in coconut milk. This is what I had longed for all these months: the love of the family and community and fresh food. I was no longer alone in a room or sitting in front of a television, but continuously surrounded by loved ones.

The first few days passed so quickly that I did not even leave the house. However, the novelty of my being home soon passed. Everyone resumed his or her daily routine. Gyan and I finally ventured into to Suva. I dressed in short pants and the traditional island shirt, and Gyan proudly put on the clothes that I had brought. As we boarded the bus in front of the house, people began shaking Gyan's hand and waving and shouting hello. Gyan was very well known in the community. Both of us proudly sat back and rode into town.

It was incredibly fulfilling to ride the bus and pass through the areas that had been my stomping grounds. Throughout the four-mile ride into town, I saw individuals that I recognized and called out to them. Some of my friends could not believe that it was actually me who was shouting out of the bus window when we passed through Samabula. The saying "out of sight, out of mind" was never truer than at this moment. Some family and friends whom we met in town didn't even recognize me until Gyan asked if they knew who I was.

Walking around the familiar streets of Suva, I noticed that a majority of the people kept asking Gyan when he arrived and when he was going back. At first, it seemed odd, but the mystery was solved during a conversation with a distant relative. He shook hands with both Gyan and me, and then proceeded to converse with Gyan while ignoring me. He asked, "So how is America? How long are you going to stay in Suva, and when are you going back?"

Because of the way he was dressed, people thought he was the one who had returned from America. Gyan answered all the questions and engaged in conversations as if he was the one who had gone away. At no time did either one of us attempt to correct anyone's assumptions. Gyan enjoyed the attention and found great enjoyment in talking about America.

All I cared about was being home and not having to worry about the name-calling or loneliness. Life for me was back to normal. We went fishing, played soccer, and enjoyed the cuisine at family gatherings. Oh yes, this was what life was all about in the Islands. America was a distant memory now. I even thought about writing to Len and informing him that I wasn't going back to the United States. How could I leave this easy-going, great life and go back to the lonely place? Yes, in a few weeks, I would inform my family about my intentions.

# Chapter Fifteen: A Dose of Reality

In a few weeks, the novelty and fame began to wane. Family and friends went back to their daily routines of school and work. On most weekdays, I found myself at home with just my mother. If I wanted to explore areas that I had not seen before or visit someone, I either had to do it alone or wait until the weekend. Since I was adventurous, I had no problem hopping on the bus and visiting places or heading for the beach. It was thrilling going on winding roads into remote jungle areas on a bus that had no windows but tarpaulin to protect us from the rain. I would stick my head out and feel the wind pass through my hair. To me, this was freedom: going where I wanted to go, doing what I wanted to do, and not having to worry about anything in the world.

Well, I had to come down to earth from my euphoria sooner or later. During a daily family conversation one evening, it became clear to me that my brothers and sisters envied me for going to America. They could not wait for me to finish my schooling and sponsor them to the "Promised Land."

Gyan was a mechanic. His dream was to go to America and work on the big, fancy American cars. "I wish I could go back with you. There is nothing here in Fiji for us. I want to sleep in a bed, not on the floor, and drive an American car." Others in the family echoed his wishes. They all wanted to leave Fiji and go to America in search of a better life. Bhai said, "Things are very difficult right now. We don't even have enough money to finish building this house or to put in electricity."

It dawned on me that I had been looking at my homeland through rose-colored glasses. While I was dreaming about the beauty of the Islands and family life, my family was waiting for me to take them away from their hard life. What I considered fun, to them was drudgery. Americans went camping to swim in the river, cook outside, and sleep under the stars. In Fiji, every day was like camping. We slept on the ground in the dark, cooked outside, walked to most places, and swam in the river or the ocean. One of my relatives stated, "You are the lucky one. The white man took you to heaven while we are all left here to toil in the soil. When you go back, do not forget those of us with old tired bones who have to sleep on the hard ground and wander around in the dark."

I had been home for three weeks, and although I enjoyed every moment, I recognized that there was no way I could stay. My five-year-old sister, Angela, who stuck to me like glue, asked me every day to take her with me. Whenever she saw an airplane in the sky, she would turn and say, "Munna brother is taking me to America on that airplane. I am going to go to school with him." Angela wanted to go everywhere I went. At night, she slept on the floor with me in the living room. She was only five, but could speak her mind in a very articulate manner. If my mother scolded her, she would let her know emphatically, "I am going to America, so you won't be able to yell at me or punish me. Munna will take care of me."

Even my baby sister looked upon me as the "savior." After listening to Angela, it was evident that any attempts to describe the harsh realities of living in the United States would be fruitless. America was God's country, and anyone who said anything against it was blasphemous. If I remained,

I would be looked upon as being a failure, someone who threw away the opportunity of a lifetime.

The time had come for me to face reality. Since my departure from Fiji, the family had somewhat changed, or perhaps it was me who had changed. Nevertheless, one thing was quite clear: It was time to stop dreaming and face reality. While I lived in the past, those around me had moved on. Time had stood still for me from the day I left the Islands for America. A stark realization hit me like a brick falling on my head. All the people around me, including the surroundings, had changed. Some of my old schoolmates had already quit school and were working. They could not afford to go to school and had to secure jobs to help their families.

I was constantly reminded about how lucky I was to have had the opportunity to migrate to America instead of having to labor in the fields or work at a menial job. Maybe I was a selfish teenager who did not realize or want to accept the responsibility that had been placed on me. As a typical teenager, I wanted nothing more than to hang out and spend my time being lazy. However, my family looked at me as the "savior" who would someday lead them to the "Promised Land," America.

Needless to say, time appeared to move slowly for the rest of the summer. I was scheduled to return to the United States at the beginning of September, in four more weeks. Perhaps it was my imagination, but the four weeks seemed like four months. There were times when I found myself wishing that I had not come back. When people greeted me, the first question out of their mouths was, "When are you going back?" Were they telling me to go back and stop wasting time in Fiji? I was perplexed. As the old saying goes, "One cannot ride two canoes down the river." I guess I was attempting to ride two canoes and being split apart.

# Chapter Sixteen: Back to the USA

One morning, my brother Gautam looked at me and quietly asked, "Are you looking forward to going back?"

My eyes became watery. I did not know how to respond. I was torn between staying and going back. "To tell you the truth, at first I did want to stay in Fiji because I am lonely in America. People make fun of me, call me names, and I always feel out of place. Now I want to go back because I also feel out of place here. Everyone seems to have changed. I feel like a guest here now, rather than a member of the family."

Gautam looked astonished at my statements. "You don't have to go back if you are unhappy there. Forget about what these people think," he responded.

Gautam was only twenty-three years old, but he possessed the wisdom of a forty-year-old. He did not have the advantages that I was being given. During his junior year in high school, he withdrew to get a job and help the family. If he had lived in the United States, Gautam would have been a scholar athlete. He was academically astute and a great athlete. He understood my quandary and did not want to place undue pressure on me. However, he was quite transparent in his opinion about what he would do if he were in my position.

Two more days and I would be boarding the plane to leave again. Few friends dropped by to say goodbye. The atmosphere was not at all like eighteen months ago when I first left. The novelty had worn off. Instead of a busload of people coming to see me off at the airport, only ten were present. Nevertheless, the parting scene was still filled with sorrow, with family members crying and hugging me so tightly as if to say, "We do not want you to go." I guess when the moment of departure becomes eminent, emotions overpower all rational thinking.

On the plane heading back to my adopted homeland, I was not afraid, sick, or overly sad. As I settled into my seat, I peeked through the tiny window and waved as the plane slowly made its way down the runway. In a short time, the engines roared and the plane moved faster and faster until it lifted off the ground headed for the sky. I looked down at the rapidly disappearing island and the blue ocean. I tilted back my seat, closed my eyes, and fell asleep.

I was looking forward to spending another week in Hawaii. I could not wait to see the Thompsons and go surfing on Waikiki Beach. Similar to the first trip, the Thompson family came to meet me at the airport and greeted me with open arms.

My week in Honolulu was filled with excitement. I spent a majority of my time surfing and exploring the area surrounding Honolulu. From what I saw, Hawaii was similar to Fiji, except it was developed and had all the modern amenities. The beaches were beautiful with warm, blue water, white sand, and palm trees swaying with the gentle trade winds. Nevertheless, all good things end quickly. Before I knew it, my week had gone by, and it was time to head for Los Angeles.

Saying goodbye to the Thompsons was not easy. They had shown me such caring and compassion as if I was one of their own children. Places have their beauties, but it is the people who make the difference. I truly believe that their compassion had a positive impact on the manner in which I looked at people and places.

Emerging from the immigration line at the Los Angeles Airport, I could see Len and Warren eyeing passengers as they came around the turn. Len spotted me and hollered, "Dhyan, welcome back." Warren shook my hand and grabbed the small bag I was carrying. Len put his arm around my waist as we proceeded to walk toward the baggage claim area. The excitement in Len's eyes and the big smile was clearly an expression of joy and love. I knew that Len loved me, but it was at this moment that I recognized how much.

In the car, Len turned to me, placed his hand on my lap, and said, "I was afraid we were not going to see you again. We thought that you wanted to stay with your family. It was a pleasant surprise to receive your telegram letting us know when you were returning."

I could not say much except smile and reply, "I am glad to be back."

I felt an excitement about being back that I could not understand. Instead of seeing mango and palm trees, I was looking at tall buildings. My mind was wandering in all directions. I was in a dream world and did not even hear the questions Len and Warren were asking about my trip. Finally, I described my experiences from the time of my arrival at Nadi to the time I left. While telling the story, I experienced a certain degree of nostalgia.

Once again, I was being torn apart by my wishes. On one hand, I was glad to be back in the United States, and on the other, I already missed home. It is best to say that I was confused about what I wanted. In essence, I wanted the comforts of America and the beauty, easy lifestyle, and companionship of my family. Yes, but I had also faced the reality in Fiji and clearly understood the expectations of my family. I was sent to receive an education and to help others realize their dreams of migrating and living the "good life." My future had been decided, and I had to make the best of the situation.

The car pulled into the long familiar driveway. There it was, the green house at the back of the driveway where I had my own room, bed, and all the comforts anyone could ask for. So, why was I feeling queasy? Subconsciously, I was afraid to face the people at school. I knew and understood what awaited me in the real world outside of the shelter of Len and the friends in the neighborhood. I did not want to be called names, have my speech made fun of, and be made to feel inferior.

# Chapter Seventeen: High School

I had made many friends at the junior high school, but the high school was going to be different. It was bigger, and students from three different junior high schools attended Glendale High. I was afraid to start all over again. Maybe my fears were premature. I was just being paranoid because of having spent three months in Fiji without worrying about anything. Perhaps I had regressed in my thinking.

The first day of school was hectic—new students running around everywhere looking for their classrooms, juniors and seniors greeting each other and sharing their summer experiences, teachers telling some students about the over-enrollment in their classes and for them to go and see their counselors. The day was half over, and I had not seen too many of my friends. Garcie and I had walked together, so I felt comfortable knowing one familiar face. As luck would have it, Garcie and I had English and physical education classes together.

When the bell rang to go to lunch, a mad rush ensued to get into the cafeteria and the outside lines for certain food items. I dashed out and secured my place in a line. Suddenly, the line was not moving as rapidly as it was in the beginning. Some of us began to wonder what was causing the problem. I stepped out for quick glimpse and saw that other students were walking up to the front and cutting in line. Several students attempted to block these bullies, only to be pushed out or threatened with bodily harm.

Several athletic-looking students attempted to force their way in front of me. I quietly explained to them that they had to wait like the rest of us. One of them, who appeared to be the leader, shouted, "Shut up, black boy. You are the one who belongs at the back of the line."

"No, I have waited a long time, and you are not going to cut in front of me."

He pushed me out of the line, and I pushed him right back. We began fighting. His friends encouraged him to "beat the crap out of the little nigger." I stood my ground, and although I did not win the fight, I did prevent them from cutting in front of us. One of the vice principals witnessed the fight and immediately intervened. He told the other boys to get in the back of the line and to see him at the end of the lunch period.

After I purchased my lunch, I found Garcie and some of my other friends from the junior high school eating their lunch on a bench under a tree. They saw the look of anger on my face and inquired about the scowl. I told them about the incident in the food line. Art commented, "I had a similar incident, but it did not lead to a fight." We agreed that the juniors and seniors were throwing around their weight and intimidating the incoming underclassmen. I did not say anything to the others about the racial slur.

On the way home, I shared the specific details of the incident that occurred in the lunch line with Garcie. He became angry and replied, "You should have found me, and we would have kicked the shit out of those guys."

"I know, but I was taken by surprise. I did not expect this kind of crap to continue at the high school."

"We should always hang out together and meet at the same location under the tree during the breaks. I know these guys like to pick on the new students. A couple of them tried to pick a fight with me in the hallway," Garcie added.

After the first couple of days, we became accustomed to the way of life in high school. One thing that all incoming freshmen learned very quickly was not to go into the senior glen. This was a grassy area with a water fountain reserved exclusively for the seniors. Once, an unsuspecting tenth-grade student wandered into the senior quad. He was picked up by a few of the boys and thrown into the water fountain. This incident sent a clear message to all of us to keep clear or suffer the consequences.

I was a little premature in my thinking that the high-school students would be more sensitive and mature. In some of the classrooms and on the physical education field, I quickly discovered that racism was eagerly raising its ugly head again. The classroom situation was similar to the one I had experienced in the junior high school. In a number of classes, students laughed when I spoke. The teachers did little or nothing to discourage the individuals from displaying such behaviors. I tried not to pay attention to the students who chose to make fun of me, but sometimes it was difficult to ignore the blatant insulting remarks.

During football practice, I was rushing to sack the quarterback. My speed made my quest successful. At one point, I turned around and saw Gary, a player from the other team, block his own man and knock him to the ground. It was unusual to see a player take his own teammate down and hinder him from blocking the rusher. After all, this was football, and preventing the opposing team members from getting to the quarterback was the offensive linemen's job. By hitting his own player, Gary permitted me to sack his quarterback.

Afterward, Gary told me why he blocked his own team member. "You kept getting to the quarterback and disrupting our plays. In the huddle, one of the players said, 'We need to take that nigger out.' So, they told me to hit you from the front and the other guy to hit you from the back. I hit my own man so he couldn't hit you from the back and hurt you. They wanted to break your leg." Gary continued, "Yeah, the other guy said for me to hit you in the mouth, and he would hit you in the back. They didn't know that I knew you and I was not going to let them hurt you. Man, my team was pissed at me for what I did, but I told them that I wasn't going to purposely hurt anyone."

Gary had moved to Glendale from Indiana at the beginning of the school year and was living with his older brother and his wife. He had a few friends, but it was quite clear that he did not choose his friends based on how they looked. From that moment, Gary and I became friends. I introduced him to all my friends, and he began to hang out with us.

High-school years were fun and busy. I gave up playing football because Garcie had quit and was working part-time after school. If Garcie didn't play football, then I didn't want to be out there alone. I asked, "Can I get a part-time job like yours?"

Garcie said, "You can work with my brother-in-law at the International House of Pancakes in Toluca Lake. I'll ask him if there is an opening." The next day, Garcie said he had some information about the job.

"What did you find out?" I asked.

"My brother-in-law Victor said that there is an opening in Toluca Lake for a dishwasher. You can work there Friday nights and all day Saturdays and Sundays."

"Yes, tell him I want to work there."

I had my first job in America. I was hired as a dishwasher at the IHOP in Toluca Lake. Garcie worked at the Encino IHOP that was about fifteen miles from Glendale. He had recently turned sixteen and bought a used Ford Fairlane. He said he would drop me off before going to his destination. On Friday, as soon as school let out, we hopped into Garcie's car and headed for work. I could not wait to start my job.

On the way, Garcie spoke to me about the position, what to expect from other workers, and some of the terminology used in the restaurant business. I was an eager beaver, paying attention to his every word. The last thing I wanted to do was start my first job with mistakes. Garcie had been working for over a month, so he was a veteran. He was a busboy and a cook's helper. The dishwasher's position was the entry-level position. I didn't care about anything because I was thrilled about earning money and not bothering Len for every little penny.

When Victor saw Garcie's Fairlane pull up, he yelled, "Hey, Manny. Come on in." He extended his hand to me saying, "You must be Dhyan."

"Yes, nice to meet you, and thank you for finding me this job."

Victor laughed. "Oh, you'll work all right. Follow me, and I'll introduce you to the manager." We walked from the back of the kitchen to the front of the restaurant.

The manager, Al, welcomed me and gave me some papers to fill out. "As soon as you are finished, I will show you your workstation, and the other dishwasher will help you get started," Victor said.

Garcie bid me goodbye and went off to his job. Victor introduced me to the cooks, waitresses, busboys, and the other dishwasher, Mitch. All the workers joked with Victor, and he gave them a hard time. Victor was the chief cook and assistant manager. He was cordial, humorous, and extremely hardworking. Sometimes he worked seven days a week putting in twelve-hour days. His hard work paid off. Ten years later, Victor bought an IHOP of his own in Bakersfield and now owns three in the greater Bakersfield area.

Walking into the pancake house was like entering a whole different world. The workers were of different races and colors. I was introduced to the first black American I'd met, Mitch. I also met people from Cuba, Mexico,

Guatemala, and the other parts of the United States. The environment and the people here were quite different from what I encountered in Glendale. All the people were very friendly, always laughing and joking. Nobody cared about how the other person looked as long as he did his job.

Mitch was an older person, perhaps in his late forties. He explained to me in great detail how to rinse the dishes, the proper water temperature to use, and to make sure that I wore gloves to prevent myself from being burned. He had been working there for five years and took pride in his work. Mitch made $1.75 an hour. This pay rate was not bad for a dishwasher in 1964. Since I was new and worked part-time, I was paid $1.25 an hour. The pay did not matter; I was happy to have a job.

I worked for four years at IHOP. On some weekends, I worked a total of thirty-two hours. I worked my way up from dishwasher to a busboy to a cook's helper. Garcie joined me as a busboy during the summer and went on to become a cook. We enjoyed working the evening shift during the summer because then we could wake up early and go to the beach. We worked sixty hours a week during the summer months, but still found time to go body surfing at Sorrento, Will Rogers, or Zuma Beach.

Although I did not participate in sports activities while I worked, I did like running. During my junior year, I spoke to the track coach and asked if I could run the mile. The coach asked me to run a few laps while he kept my time. He told me to run every day during my physical education class. Garcie and I were in the same class, so we provided friendly competition for each other. Garcie always beat me in the 50-, 100-, and 200-yard races. However, I won the 400-yard, 880-yard, and the mile races. Garcie was strong and had quick starts, whereas I had a slow start, but kept a steady pace.

I qualified to run in the 880-yard meet for the school. On the day of the race, the football stadium was packed with students. When the gun sounded, I took off like a racehorse and sprinted far ahead of all my competitors. I could hear a few of my friends cheering for me as I turned the first corner. The 880-yard, or half-mile, race was very grueling, but I was sure that I was going to run the two laps with no problem. I completed the first lap in fifty-five seconds. The other boys were a good ten yards behind me. With only a hundred yards left to go, I was certain that I was going to win. Suddenly, I felt an excruciating pain shooting from my right calf. I could not put my leg down without feeling severe pain. I had a cramp in the right calf muscle.

I was hopping on one foot. The other boys began to pass me one by one. As they passed me, the crowd cheered loudly. I finished the race in last place. The audience laughed as I passed by. Yes, that ugliness of prejudice came through loud and clear. My friends applauded me, but the laughter of the majority drowned their encouragement. The coach placed his arm around my shoulder and asked if I was okay. He placed an ice pack on my calf and advised me to drink plenty of water.

The pain in my stomach overshadowed the pain in my leg. I was sad, mad, and disgusted. I wanted to win because I knew that by winning, I would shut up those smart-aleck, condescending people who didn't think I could beat the white kids. Not only did I lose, but I came in last. The pain in my stomach was from the laughter I kept hearing in my head. How could I lose? I should have skipped work and trained harder after school. Now, instead of walking away with the first-place trophy, I was hobbling off the field in disgrace being helped by Garcie and Gary.

On the way home, I kept hitting the dashboard with my fist in anger. Garcie attempted to console me, but to no avail. In his calm way, he said, "If it wasn't for the cramp, you would have beat the other guys by ten yards and finished under two minutes. They didn't beat you; they won because you got hurt." Garcie was always cool and the voice of reason. However, right now, I was not in the mood to listen. I was mad at myself for not winning and, above all, for placing myself in a predicament that allowed others to laugh at me. "You want to go to Bob's and get a Coke and a Big Boy?" Garcie asked.

"No, just take me home. I want to go to sleep."

The scene of the crowd laughing at me as I hobbled across the finish line played like a tape recorder in my mind over and over. I could not get over the humiliation. It took a long time for me to put the event of that day out of my mind and concentrate on the following year. I made a promise to myself that I would not be in this predicament again.

Garcie transferred from the Encino IHOP to the Toluca Lake restaurant. I began working on Wednesday nights in addition to Friday nights, Saturday all day, and Sunday. Sometimes we worked sixteen hours straight. Nevertheless, working with a great group of people made the time spent at the workplace enjoyable. Often Garcie and I competed to see who could clean a table the fastest or attend to other duties without sacrificing our initial job of clearing and cleaning the tables.

What we looked forward to were the meals the cooks would make for us. In the mornings, we could eat and drink whatever we wanted. The restaurant opened at seven, and we had to arrive early to make coffee and orange juice, and make sure that all the tables were set properly. If the restaurant was not too busy, we took turns eating. Len and I were living alone and did not cook much at home, so eating at work was not only desirable, it became a necessity.

Len did not like the idea of my working on school nights, but I promised him that my schoolwork would not suffer. He was proud that I wanted to pay for everything and not be a burden on him, but he also instilled in me that education came before anything. So, when I received a less-than-satisfactory notice from the science teacher, Len became very angry and demanded that I quit my job immediately and concentrate on my studies. My grades in all my classes were not great, but I did receive Bs and Cs with As in physical education. I reassured him that I would improve and if I did not, I would stop working. Len agreed, albeit reluctantly.

At the end of the junior year, I received Cs and Bs and of course an A in physical education. I was proud to let Len know that rather than failing the science class, I received a B in it. He was happy that I kept my promise, but reminded me, "A smart boy like you should not be getting any Cs. I know that you are still getting used to the language and fighting other problems, but by studying harder you could do better."

I became defensive and responded like a spoiled teenager, "Well, I am doing the best I can. There are guys who are getting Ds and Fs, and they are Americans."

Len gave me his familiar smile and replied, "I just want the best for you."

I had attended summer school the year before, but asked Len if I could skip summer school and work full-time this year. He was a little hesitant at first, but gave in to my request. Garcie and I had already secured a full-time position at the IHOP. I immediately called Garcie. "Len said it was okay for me to work full-time. Now we can work at night and go to the beach in the daytime." We had our summer planned. This was going to be a summer filled with fun.

Before we knew it, the summer was over. We had a great time going to the beach, playing football and soccer, and hanging out. The amount of time we spent working didn't matter because we were making money.

No longer were Garcie and I the two funny-looking kids from faraway places. We both had our drivers' licenses. Garcie had his own car, and I could use Len's Ford Falcon station wagon anytime I wanted to. And we took full advantage of the station wagon; we used it to carry our surfboards to the beach.

Surfing was popular in the United States, especially in Southern California. Everyone was learning how to surf. The Beach Boys, the hottest group in the United States, had released their new song, "Surfing U.S.A.," which became number one almost overnight. Since I was from the "Islands," my buddies assumed that I was a good surfer. I did not dissuade them from thinking otherwise. I was pretty good, but not like the image my buddies had of me on a surfboard.

# Chapter Eighteen: Is High School Over?

It dawned on me that this was the last year of high school. I could not believe that I had been in America for almost four years. My thoughts about going back to Fiji had diminished as time passed. However, there still were times when I wondered what I would be doing if I hadn't left the Islands and if the rest of the family still missed me. Our correspondence had decreased from writing every other day to once a week to every other week or longer. I had become totally engrossed in my school and outside activities. There was little time to be lonely or feel sorry for myself.

The first day of school was thrilling. We were the big, bad seniors now. All the guys were dressed in the latest fashion with hair longer than usual, the Beatles' influence, and the girls had the Annette Funicello, the star in all the beach party movies, hairstyle. It appeared as if the whole school had gone shopping and bought new clothes. My friend Art had bought a car, and another friend, Ken, had worked with his father in construction and bought himself a Woody. Everyone had an interesting story to share about the summer vacation. There was an atmosphere of vitality throughout the campus. During the lunch break, the entire campus was filled with noise, laughter, hugging, and sounds of "Good to see you; how was your summer?"

We were the seniors, the big dogs on campus. Now we could hang out in the senior glen without having to suffer the consequences. However, we were all creatures of habit and hung out at our usual place under the tree. The same group of guys met every day, ate lunch, and then ventured off to play basketball. Garcie and I were better at football and soccer than basketball. The football coach wanted us to play on the high-school football team, but because both of us worked after school, we could not. In retrospect, I wish I had played in high school and college. I had the speed to run routes as a wide receiver and hands to catch the ball.

One day while I was walking to my government class, a girl stopped me and asked me a question about the teacher because she was going to have him the following semester. Her name was Randi, and she was from Norway. Our conversation went beyond the questions about the class to where she was hanging out during lunch and if she would like to continue our conversation after school. To my surprise, she said, "I would love to meet you, but I am helping an exchange student from Norway after school."

"Bring her along," I responded. The bell began ringing, and we both dashed into our respective classrooms.

I could not wait to tell Garcie about my conversation with Randi. As soon as the bell for nutrition rang, I hurried to our usual hangout to look for Garcie and tell him the good news. "Hey, Garce, you will not believe what happened to me on my way to the first-period class."

"What?" he asked.

"Well, this cute girl stopped me and started asking me questions about my government class, and I asked her if she would like to meet me after school, and she said yes."

Garcie laughed. "Yeah right, a cute girl's gonna meet you after school. Wake up, Dhyan, you are dreaming."

"Okay, don't believe me; just meet me at the usual place after school."

Randi; her friend from Norway, Britt; and I walked out of the building to meet Garcie. I saw him as we were walking down the stairs, but he was looking in the other direction. "Hey, Garce," I hollered. He turned around, and there was a look of astonishment on his face. I, on the other hand, had an arrogant look.

Before I could say anything, Garcie smiled and held out his hand. "Hi, I am Manuel."

I chimed in, "This is Randi, and this is Britt, an exchange student from Norway. They are going to join us for root beer floats at the A&W."

Garcie gave me a look that said, "I didn't know we were going to the root beer place."

There were a few minutes of silence while we were sipping on our floats. I asked Britt, "So, how long have you been in the country?"

She replied, "Two weeks." She spoke English with an accent that I had never before heard.

We spoke about our respective countries and the differences between our homelands and America. Randi said that her family left Norway when she was eight years old and had been back once. "I miss the snow and skiing, but life was hard for us back home." Her father did not want to migrate, so he decided to stay in Norway. Randi's mother brought her and her sister, hoping that her husband would change his mind and follow them. He never did come to the United States.

Garcie, Britt, Randi, and I began to go out places together and even went on dates. Whenever the four of us walked down the streets of Glendale, people would turn their heads and stare at us. We knew that seeing the two of us was unusual, but to see us with white girls intensified the people's curiosity.

There were times when we overheard individuals make snide remarks or even derogatory comments. Once, when we came out of a movie, two men passed us by and said, "Look at them two niggers with white girls. They must be whores."

Garcie became enraged and pushed one of them and asked, "What did you say? You want to do something about it?" I quickly pulled Garcie back and told the two to move on. They were petrified by Garcie's response and moved quickly away from us. The usually cool and calm Garcie was pissed and ready to kill.

The girls were visibly shaken by what had just happened. They assured us that they did not care about what people thought because they had fun going out with us. Our relationship lasted until the end of high school, when all of us went our separate ways. Britt went back to Norway, Randi went off to a university, and Garcie and I enrolled at Glendale Community College.

High-school years had passed us by quickly. Only three months were left before graduation. I was satisfied with my academic and social life. However, one scenario kept playing in my mind: the laughter of the spectators when I came in last in the half-mile race during the track meet. The humiliation was unbearable, and I made myself a promise that I would run the race again and do everything in my power to win.

It was a warm day in May, and the entire stadium was filled with cheering students. A school-wide track and field competition was being held to honor all the athletes and provide them an opportunity to show their athletic prowess. I entered to run the half-mile race. Three weeks before the competition, I ran at least one mile every day at full speed to prepare myself. Now it was time for me to redeem myself and quiet the crowd who laughed so loudly at me the previous year. Yes, the black boy of the high school was ready to show that he was not inferior.

The runners lined up on the track and took their positions in the starting blocks waiting for the gun to sound. Even after four years in the country, I could not feel comfortable with running shoes and still ran barefoot. Kneeling and positioning myself in the blocks, I looked up at the crowd and could see some students pointing at me and laughing. No doubt, they were making reference to my bare feet and probably my dismal performance the previous year. I lowered my head, closed my eyes, and concentrated on my inner self.

When I lifted my head, the official had raised his starting pistol and was ready to yell the familiar words, "ready, set," before firing the gun. The sound of the gun made us leap forward and run like a thundering herd of cattle during a stampede. I vaulted forward and began running with all the energy and speed my legs could muster. I finished the first 400 meters at least thirty yards ahead of my closest competitor. This scene was reminiscent of the previous year when I was the leader of the pack during the first half of the race. I knew that I could not slow down and had to maintain my speed at all costs.

Suddenly, I felt a slight tingle in my right calf. I didn't pay attention to the calf, and it was becoming painful with each step. With only 100 yards left in the race, the pain became excruciating. I looked back and saw that the pack had closed the gap. The second-place person was approximately ten yards behind and closing in on me at a rapid pace. I closed my eyes and ran, imagining myself flying through space with the wind pushing.

The cheer of the crowd became louder, luring me to open my eyes. To my astonishment, I was crossing the ribbon, finishing the race in first place. My closest competitor was about four yards behind me. I immediately fell to the ground with tears of joy and pain in my eyes. Finally, victory was mine, and the very individuals who had jeered at me now cheered for me.

I brought the first-place trophy home and showed it to Len. He was elated. He gave me a hug saying, "That's my boy." Watching the proud look on Len's face made me even more ecstatic about winning.

Garcie filled Len in with the details of the race. "Dhyan took off like a horse and was ahead of everybody, but then he began to slow down. I was afraid he may not finish the race because he was hobbling. All of a sudden, he picked up speed again like he got a second wind and won the race."

I told them about the cramp in my leg, but that my desire to win made me run like a man possessed. "All I could see and hear was the people pointing at me and the laughter. I was determined to redeem myself at any cost."

Graduation day was only two weeks away. The students were cramming for their finals. Hallways were buzzing with students talking about what colleges they had been accepted to and where they chose to attend. Some of the students were afraid of leaving home and venturing off to faraway places. Those of us who had already decided to attend a community college did not have to make complex decisions or worry about leaving home. The only thing worrying me was passing the government class.

One could not graduate without passing this compulsory class. On the last day of class, the teacher was passing back the final term paper. He asked me to stay after class. I was terrified. Students who were asked to stay after class or after school were those who were in trouble.

I timidly approached Mr. Andrews' desk. He was arranging the papers that had piled on his desk. "You wanted to see me, Mr. Andrews," I softly mumbled while trembling.

"Yes, I wanted to ask you where you acquired the information for your term paper on unions. Some of facts you mention are not in any books or magazines. What is the source of your information?"

"Well, sir, my guardian was one of the organizers of the Congress of Industrial Organization (CIO). He worked with John L. Lewis, the founder of the CIO, and was the editor of the union newspaper," I replied. "I received the bulk of the information from my guardian, Len De Caux."

Mr. Andrews smiled. "You did a great job. You have an A on the term paper, and if you did well on the final, you may receive a B in the class." This was the first time I had seen Mr. Andrews smile.

Most of us could not wait to get out of high school, but now we all felt remorseful about leaving the place that had become our home for three years. Graduation time was at two o'clock. The girls had their hair done and were dressed in pretty dresses. Most of the boys wore suits, and some even donned tuxedos. A stage with microphones and chairs was placed on the football field. The stadium bleachers were packed with family and friends of the graduates. We marched in to the graduation music, "Pomp and Circumstance," and took our places on the field as we had practiced. The crowd cheered loudly, hollering the names of graduates. Graduation speakers arose from their seats one by one and delivered their speeches.

Some of the adult speakers tended to be long-winded, causing restlessness among the graduates. Finally, we heard the principal announce that it was time to hand the diplomas to the students. One by one, we walked onto the stage gingerly to accept our diplomas and pause for pictures. A majority of us were too self-conscious and could not wait to get off the stage. When the last name was announced, a loud roar engulfed the stadium area. Caps were hurled in the air with deafening cheers. Family and friends piled onto the field carrying flowers and gifts. Laughter and crying could be seen in every direction. After all, this was the absolute finale: There was no tomorrow in high school.

Len and some friends from the neighborhood navigated their way through the crowd to greet and congratulate Garcie and me. He had that familiar smile on his face that said, "I am proud of you, my son." I was elated because I had completed a milestone and, above all, because I had made Len happy.

Here was a man who brought me to America without any guarantees as to how I would perform in schools or how I would behave once I was away from the family. Four years later, the little boy from the village had graduated from an American high school. This was not a dream; it was reality.

# Chapter Nineteen: Returning to Paradise

All through high school, I had worked at the pancake house. I routinely sent money home to help the family and make sure that my brother and sister stayed in school. Yet, I managed to save enough money for a vacation. I had told my boss that I would not be working during the summer. He advised me that there were no guarantees of a job for me after the summer. I thanked him for being kind enough to allow me to work there for the past three years. Many of the workers were sad to see me leave because we had formed a bond, much like a family. I told them that I was going home to Fiji and would come back in September. Some of the workers brought clothes and other items for me to take back.

One week after graduation, Len drove me to the Los Angeles Airport, and I was on my way. It was 1966; four and half years had passed since I first stepped out of the airplane at the same airport. Now I was making my second journey back. Unlike the trip in 1963, when I couldn't wait to leave the United States, this time I had conflicting feelings. I wanted to go home, and at the same time, I was sad about leaving Len and my friends.

As the plane lifted from the ground and headed for the clouds, climbing higher and higher, I realized that the feeling in my stomach was similar to the one I had felt when I first departed Fiji. Now I was a man with two homes and families. The humming of the engines of the plane was intoxicating, and I drifted into a deep sleep.

Stepping out of the plane at Nadi airport and smelling the fresh air and feeling the warm breeze reminded me of what I had missed. I quickly grabbed a cab and was on my way to Suva. The family knew that I was coming, but they had no idea when. Once again, I was going to surprise them with a knock on the door in the early hours of the morning. The taxi pulled in front of the house at about five o'clock in the morning.

After two knocks on the door, I could hear someone yelling, "Munna is here." He opened the door and immediately embraced me saying, "I knew you were coming today or tomorrow."

Before long, everyone came flying out of the rooms, some still putting on their shirts while others were tying the "sulu." Bhai approached, held me in his arms, and said, "Welcome back, good to have you home, son." Then he turned around uttered, "Make some tea and bring food; the boy must be hungry after a long travel. See, I told you last night when the plane flew over the house that Munna is on that plane."

Bhai had a way of predicting events that usually came to fruition. Of course, I did not arrive on the plane that had passed overhead, but he was right about my arrival. The living room was packed with the whole family asking questions and going through the suitcases and boxes that I had brought to find their gifts. This scenario was a repeat of what had occurred in 1963. Times like these reminded me that no amount of materialistic comforts can replace the love of a family. I was fortunate enough to have two loving families while there are people who have none.

Similar to my last visit in 1963, I was a celebrity for a short while until my guest status wore off. Numerous events had transpired since my last visit. Gautam and my oldest sister, Shri Mati, whom we called Lalli, had both gotten married. Since Gautam was the eldest, it was his duty to help bhai with the family. Lalli, however, had moved away with her husband's family.

Shortly after my arrival, Lalli and her husband, Ramesh, departed for a visit to Australia. They left their two-year-old son, Binnu, behind with amma to babysit. Somehow, I was drafted into being the alternate babysitter and was given the responsibility of watching Binnu when amma was busy with her chores.

Babu was twenty years old, had a driver's license, and was employed as a mechanic. He was proud of his abilities and wanted to migrate to the United States to pursue his trade. We capitalized on his mechanical abilities by renting old cars and touring the island. If the cars had problems, Babu was usually able to repair them. We frequented remote areas that had waterfalls, streams, thick rain forests, and pristine beaches. Sometimes there were eight of us crammed in a car.

During one of the outings, we saw a soccer team practicing. We stopped and joined the team members. The teams in the various towns and villages were preparing for the annual inter-district soccer tournament. This was the biggest annual sporting event. Babu and I decided to practice with the team every day to see if we could qualify for the team. Much to our surprise, both of us made the final cut and were selected to play on the team. Unfortunately for me, bhai would not let me play because he was afraid that I would break my leg or injure myself in some way and not be able to return to America.

One day, as we were sitting in the living room and talking, Babu glanced at me and said, "You are so lucky to be able to travel. I want to visit New Zealand, but can't earn enough money for the plane fare."

I had some money, so I asked, "How much do you need?"

"Well, I have $100, and I need at least $200 more for the fare," he replied.

"Don't worry; I can give you the money you need," I assured him. Babu was ecstatic and immediately consulted the calendar to see the best time for him to depart for his journey. He wanted to leave soon after my return to America.

# Chapter Twenty: The College Years

Someone said, "Time flies when you are having fun." Truer words were never spoken. Before I knew it, it was time to pack my bags and head back to the United States. Although I knew that I had to go back to America and resume my education, I did not want to leave. I had become accustomed to the routine of waking every morning to the sounds of birds chirping and the sun shining through the window, taking a shower, eating freshly cooked vegetables and roti, and heading into town. I looked forward to walking through Suva, observing the people as they performed their daily tasks in a laid-back island style. In the United States, everyone was always in a rush to get somewhere or do something. Here, individuals moved about in a casual manner, stopping to speak with someone or drink a bowl of kava. This was the simple island life that I longed to enjoy, but could not because of my duty of helping the family.

While I desired the life in the Islands, my relatives coveted the life I enjoyed in America. Therefore, it was my obligation to receive an education, better my own life, and help others migrate and realize their dreams. While my heart wanted me to stay, my mind reminded me of my responsibility.

Not only was I reluctant to leave the peaceful carefree lifestyle, but I was also a bit fearful about the new adventure that awaited me: college. I was somewhat apprehensive about attending college and meeting the demands of a rigorous academic curriculum. I was not sure if I could work and continue my education. One thing was perfectly clear: I was not going to remain in Fiji. It would be ten years before I would make another trip to my beloved islands.

Back at the Los Angeles airport, Len was waiting for me as he had done previously. As soon as he saw me, he waved his hands and darted past the crowd to shake my hand. "I thought this time you really decided not to come back because you cancelled your original flight."

"No, I wanted to stay, but I know that everyone wants me to go to college and receive a good education," I responded.

"Garcie and some of your other friends have been asking about you," said Len. "They also thought that you decided to stay back."

At this moment, I really did not know what was home, Fiji or America. I was a man who was torn between two worlds—one that offered a simple life devoid of materialistic possessions and the other that had all the trappings of a future filled with unlimited resources. The choice had already been made for me that balmy night in 1961 when bhai and Len sat on the porch and discussed the possibility of me going to America to be educated. I had to make a conscious effort to put Fiji out of my mind, take the opportunity presented, and make something of myself. There is an old saying in Fiji that goes something like, "A man cannot ride in two canoes at the same time; he must choose one or the other, or he will find himself in deep trouble."

I had arrived on Saturday, and the registration for Glendale Community College was on Monday. I guess there is nothing like waiting until the last minute to enroll. Monday morning, there I was, sitting in a large auditorium with approximately four hundred other students waiting for the counselors to call my name and give me the classes. By now, all the popular classes at the convenient times had already been filled. Garcie and a few of my other friends were also in the auditorium, making the long day of waiting a bit easier.

While fooling around and playing silly games to kill time, I noticed three girls sitting in front of us who kept looking at us and making faces. I pulled the hair of one the girls. When she looked back at us, I pointed at Garcie. She looked at Garcie, and he pointed at me saying, "He pulled your hair and is trying to blame it on me." She laughed and went back to talking to her friends.

Later, I tapped the girl on the shoulder and confessed that it was me who had pulled her hair, but I did it only because my friend Garcie liked her and wanted to meet her.

She said, "I am Nancy, and who are you guys?"

"I am Dhyan, and this is my friend Manuel Garcia, and the other guy is Art." Always the gentleman, Garcie apologized for my behavior.

I was not called by the counselor after waiting for eight hours, which meant that I would have to follow the same routine the next day. Garcie, Nancy, and some of our other friends had been lucky and were called to enroll in their classes. They had registered before me and had a higher number.

The following day, I was sitting in the auditorium dressed in my bright blue, Hibiscus-flower shirt reading the class catalog. A young man who was also wearing an island print shirt approached me and asked, "Hey, you from Hawaii?"

"No, I'm from Fiji," I replied.

"My name is Butch Ramos, and I am from Hawaii. Nice to meet you." He sat down next to me, and we began exchanging stories about our homelands.

Butch had arrived from Honolulu the previous week and was living with an aunt in Los Angeles. While we were talking, we saw two more students, one male and one female, who appeared to be from the Islands. We called out to them, and they came over to where we were sitting. Indeed, both of them were from Hawaii. Warren was from the big island, and Colette was from Honolulu.

Finally, I had some people with whom I could identify because of our similar backgrounds, albeit not the same language. The island culture we shared superseded race and ethnicity. The next day, we met three other students who had come from Hawaii. We instantly formed a little clique. Our common experiences were the catalyst that bound us together. Being strangers in this new land, we needed each other for comfort and support.

Life at Glendale College was much different from that at Glendale High School. There were no bells telling us when to go to class, eat, or go home. Classes were offered from seven in the morning until ten at night. Students could take all their classes in the morning or stagger them throughout the day.

I discovered that some classes only met on Monday, Wednesday, and Friday, while others only met on Tuesday and Thursday. We had our choice of the times and days we wanted to attend. By the time I was called by the counselor, I could only sign up for the classes available, which meant that my classes would be staggered throughout the day.

Because I was a foreign student on a special visa, I was obligated to take no less than twelve units each semester. If I did not take the required units, the college would have to report my status to the U.S. Immigration and Naturalization Office, and I would be subject to deportation.

I registered for five classes, including one class that met only once a week, Monday nights from seven to ten. In the meantime, I acquired a job at a laundry mart that permitted me to work flexible hours. I worked at the laundry in between classes and on Saturdays. There were times when I was literally running back and forth.

No matter how busy I was, I always found time to party on Saturday nights. There were times that I went straight from partying all night to work. When you are young, you do crazy things and feel invincible. I met students from various countries. We established the International Students Club. The primary reason for the club was to meet people from other parts of the world and provide comfort to those who felt lonely or homesick. We also organized cultural activities to acquaint the other students with our countries and cultures.

It soon became apparent that a majority of the male members of the club had grown up playing soccer and wanted to organize a soccer team. We approached the college athletic department and received permission to start a team.

Much to my surprise, we had some extremely talented players. Our center forward, Chiat, who was from Thailand, was fast and could dribble the ball with such finesse that players from other teams were left wondering what had just sped passed them. Garcie and I chose to play defense; he played right fullback, and I took the position of left fullback. We had played together since our arrival in America and understood each other's abilities.

If a ball did get by either Garcie or me, we did not have much to worry about because our goalkeeper, George, who was from Holland, was a master at his position. We referred to him as "George the magnet." No matter where the ball was kicked, George's hands were there to catch it. Rarely did a team score a goal against us.

The first year, we finished with a record of twelve wins and three losses. However, during our second season, we played the UCLA freshman team for the Southern California championship and beat them by a score of two to one. We completed the season with only one defeat.

My class schedule changed during the second semester of school, forcing me to give up my laundry job and seek other employment. I had met a student named Chris whose family was from France. Chris used to deliver newspapers in the morning. I went along with him for a few days and learned the routine of tying papers and throwing them from the car at five in the morning.

Shortly, I had my own paper route. Well, this adventure did not last long. One cold, dark Sunday morning as I was attempting to find some apartments in a huge complex, I heard the sound of someone falling in the water. That someone happened to be me. I was stepping back to read the numbers, did not see the pool, and fell into the cold water.

I instantly ran to my car and rushed my shivering body home. While attempting to open the door, I noticed that the light inside the living room was on. Len had been awakened by the noise I was making and came out to see what was happening. "You are all wet. What happened?" he asked.

The cold had penetrated my bones and caused me to shiver so incessantly that I had difficulty answering. "I fell in a swimming pool," I shouted as I ran to my room to dry off and change my clothes.

Len was concerned about my condition and followed me into the room. He quietly looked at me for a while and finally said, "You know you don't have to work so hard day and night and go to school. You can't keep this up. Just work one job and give up this one."

I knew he was right, but at that moment, I was ashamed and too cold and tired to think. After changing, I said, "See you later," and went to finish my paper route.

Later that day, I called my supervisor and informed him that I was quitting the job. I also called my friend Chris and let him know of my decision to stop delivering the morning paper. At home that afternoon, I told Len about my decision. He was pleased to hear that I had quit and expressed his concern about my safety and well-being. Len was proud that

I wanted to be financially independent, but he did not want me to sacrifice my health or education. I assured him that I would not let anything jeopardize my schooling.

After leaving the paper delivery job, I worked at a factory on the conveyor belt taking computer papers off the belt and placing them into boxes. Although this job was not difficult, the hours were from eleven at night to seven in the morning. On Tuesdays and Thursdays, I had an eight o'clock class. I would drive home after work, take a quick shower, and dash off to my economics class.

I performed rather poorly in the economics class and barely received a C. Usually, I drank two or three cups of black coffee to stay awake. There were times, however, when I slept through the entire class. On several occasions, Gary had to give me a nudge to keep me from falling off the chair.

Finally, during my second year at Glendale College, I found a job that was satisfying and the hours flexible. Hudson Oxygen Therapy Sales Company in Los Angeles, just outside of Glendale, hired me. This company made equipment for oxygen tanks, tubes, and all other apparatus related to assisted breathing. My supervisor, Rupert Randall, was a kind and caring gentleman who took pride in showing me how to repair regulators and install them on the oxygen tanks. He liked me from the very beginning and went out of his way to teach me all about the business. Mr. Randall was pleased with the speed and efficiency with which I worked and permitted me to set my own hours. I worked at Hudson for three years until the company moved to Temecula, California.

My first year of college was challenging, to say the least. The primary reason for some of the difficulties I was experiencing in school was because of the extracurricular activities combined with my job. I had finally discovered the real life in America. No longer was I the shy little boy who cried every night, but a teenager who had made many friends and was invited to several parties every weekend. I was enjoying my newfound popularity. There were times when some of us met after school to study and wound up drinking beer most of the night. My grade point average after the first year was D+. I was called into the dean's office and placed on academic probation.

The fear of failing and disappointing Len compelled me to enroll in summer school to improve my academic standing. I registered for the morning classes so I could work in the afternoon. At the conclusion of summer school, I began working the morning shift to free the afternoons for the beach. A whole group of us would pack our coolers with beer and head for the beach.

These were wild times—the time of the British invasion, Woodstock, and the height of the hippie movement. Free concerts by popular bands and peace rallies were held at Venice Beach on weekends. There were moments when a few of us ended up sleeping on the beach or under the pier at night.

Despite all of the carousing, I managed to maintain an above-average grade point, went to work every day, and played for the school soccer team. It was during my second year that I met Dale Weiscopf. Dale was in my economics class. We made plans to study together a few times, but he rarely kept his appointments. I discovered that Dale was the assistant manager of a Jack in the Box restaurant and usually worked long hours. He was living in an apartment with a roommate. Dale was a nice but angry person. He worked to support himself and his younger brother who was living with his alcoholic parents. He rarely spoke about his family, but when we became better acquainted, he shared some of the horror stories about his life.

One day, Dale came to class late with a tired and forlorn look on his face. "What's wrong?" I asked. He turned, glared at me, and shook his head. After class, I said, "Hey, Dale, let's go for a cup of coffee."

"I can't; I have to go to work pretty soon," he replied.

"Oh hell, let's sit and talk for five minutes," I continued. He reluctantly agreed to join me. "What's wrong, Dale?" I asked. "I have noticed that you come to class late most of the time. Today, you look lost and angry."

"Oh shit, my roommate moved out, I can't afford to pay the rent by myself, and I have nowhere to go. I guess I have to drop out of school and work full-time," he replied, shaking his head and lighting a cigarette.

I didn't know what to say except, "Don't worry; something will work out."

Len liked all my friends. He had met Dale and thought that he was a very pleasant and respectful young man. On Sunday evening as we sat on the porch talking, I shared Dale's predicament with Len and asked if Dale could spend a few days with us until he found a place to live. Being the kind and generous soul that he was, Len responded, "Sure, you have an extra bed in your room. He can stay as long as he wants." I knew all along that Len would never say no when it came to helping someone.

"You know, Unkie, here I go around feeling sorry for myself because I am so far from my family, and yet there are people my age who either don't have families or have families that don't care. I am so lucky to have you. Thank you for being my dad."

Len looked up from his newspaper gave me a smile and uttered, "You're welcome."

Len continued reading his newspaper and slowly sipping on his martini. I drove over to the Jack in the Box where Dale was working and gave him the good news. At first, Dale resisted saying, "No, man, I don't want to take advantage of you and Unkie. I'll find a place." I insisted that he move in with us and continue his schooling. A week later, Dale brought his meager belongings and joined us. Between school and work, Dale and I were very busy; however, we did find time to talk late at night and during our partying on weekends.

I introduced Dale to Joyce, another one of my friends from Hawaii. Dale and Joyce instantly took a liking to each other. Joyce had been living with a roommate in a two-bedroom apartment until Nancy and her two sisters took up residence with her. Nancy's father had abandoned her and her sisters, leaving them no place to stay. Since Nancy and Garcie were dating, Nancy had joined our inner circle of island friends. When Joyce heard about Nancy's situation, she invited them to move in with her, if they did not mind sleeping on the floor.

Our circle of friends became one big family. We hung around together, supported each other however and whenever we could, and kept each other from getting into any type of trouble. All of us were struggling to maintain our grades in school and forge a life for ourselves. Despite the hardships, we all somehow managed to keep our heads above water.

# Chapter Twenty-One: Affliction of the Vietnam War

While many of us were living it up, our friends were being drafted into the armed services. The Vietnam War was at its peak. Peace marches and demonstrations to stop the killing in Vietnam and bring our young people home were being held throughout the country. Len was a pacifist. Although he had served in the First World War in the British army and as a correspondent in the Second World War in the American army, he opposed the Vietnam War. He felt that we had no right to go to a country 10,000 miles away and exert our influence on them. I shared Len's beliefs and participated in some of the peace marches. By this time, I had also grown my hair long and sported a beard.

In order to keep from being drafted, students had to carry at least twelve units and maintain good academic standing. Garcie and I both carried fifteen units. Unfortunately, Garcie was performing poorly in one of his classes and decided to withdraw from it. This was a four-unit class. Immediately after dropping the class, Garcie received a notice to report to the local draft board. He was drafted into the army. Concurrently, Dale decided that life was unbearable and joined the service, as did Gary. All at once, my friends were either being drafted or joining the service. Being a foreign student, I was not subject to the draft.

Before his departure, Garcie decided to marry Nancy. He was assigned to Bayonne, New Jersey, at the conclusion of basic training. As soon as he became settled in his new environment, Nancy joined him. Dale, however, was not as lucky. He was assigned to Germany for a short while and then shipped to Vietnam. In fact, Dale served two tours in Vietnam. He became a corporal, but was shot and badly injured during his second tour. The eighteen months Dale spent fighting in the jungles of Vietnam left him physically and mentally scarred.

I was awakened by someone yelling, "Get down, hit the deck, incoming," one night. I was startled by the noise and looked toward Dale. He was on the ground with his hands covering his head and neck, attempting to crawl under the bed.

"Dale, Dale, wake up. Are you all right?" I yelled. He did not seem to hear me. Not knowing what to do, I shook him.

He grabbed my hand with such a grip that I thought he was going to break it. Then he looked up and said, "What happened? What am I doing on the floor?"

"You were having a nightmare and screaming. I tried to wake you up, but you did not hear me. I shook you, and you grabbed my hand as if you were going to kill me." He was perplexed at what I had told him and apologized for hurting my arm.

The incident occurred at about three in the morning. We stayed awake the rest of the night talking about it. Dale described the horrors of the war and the death and destruction he had witnessed. "Listen, Fiji, there are so many things that I can't tell you because they were too horrible to describe. Man, I saw my buddies get blown away, some burned by our own guys and others stepping on booby traps. Usually when we had incoming, we ducked for cover. Raising our heads, we saw our friends lying there dead.

Some guys became so jittery that they shot at anything that moved. Gooks were everywhere. You couldn't tell who was with you and who was trying to kill you. Even women and children could not be trusted."

While telling the story, Dale placed his hand over his eyes and started crying. "I'm sorry, man," he said, "but there was so much shit going on over there that we didn't know one day from another. Half of the guys were always high on weed, and the other half were either drunk or spaced out. Sometimes it rained for weeks without stopping, and we had to crawl through rice paddies getting mud and all kinds of crap on our body.

"The first time I got shot, they patched me up and sent me back to the front lines. The second time, it was an incoming that exploded close to me, and shrapnel got all in my back and legs. It hurt and burned so bad that I wanted to die."

Listening to Dale's story reaffirmed my antiwar stance. America's youth were dying in a war that they did not understand. Vietnamese men, women, and children were being massacred by bombs dropped from the sky or guns fired from a ship. There wasn't much I could do but listen and console my friend.

I could see the rays of the sun peering through the bedroom window. We had been up half the night, and neither one of us could go back to sleep. Our conversation about the war continued over several cups of coffee. Len came out of his room and asked what the commotion was all about. We told him we couldn't sleep and decided to get up and get some coffee. He grabbed a cup of coffee and joined us. Instead of talking about the war, we changed the subject to college. Len asked Dale if he had any plans of going back to school, and Dale replied, "Yes."

Dale did not go back to school. He began working full-time and informed me that he was planning to ask Joyce to marry him. I was happy for him and Joyce. But I did have a concern about the nightmares that had not subsided. He was sleeping less and drinking whenever he was not working. Two months later, Dale found a drafting job, moved into his own apartment, and married Joyce.

I did not see Dale much after he was married, but I did speak to him on the phone a few times. Garcie informed me that Dale and Joyce had bought a house in the San Fernando Valley. They were both working, but Dale was drinking heavily and had become very distraught and negative. Joyce was extremely concerned about Dale's behavior, but he refused to go for help or listen to anyone. I decided to call Dale, but his phone had been disconnected. Later, I discovered that they had sold their house and moved to Hawaii. Joyce thought that a change of environment and support from her family might help Dale.

In the middle of the last semester of Glendale College, Butch's loneliness and homesickness overpowered his ability to cope with the life on the mainland. He called his parents and informed them that he was coming home. I was sad to see Butch depart. We had established a bond that went beyond friendship. He was always upbeat, positive, and a jokester who would say to someone who looked unhappy, "It ain't no big thing; you'll get over it." Similar to Butch, some of the other students either went home or left school to work full-time.

A few of us managed to graduate from the junior college with our Associate of Arts degrees within two years. Graduation time was bittersweet because some of our colleagues had died in Vietnam while others had been injured or remained fighting. Nevertheless, we celebrated our accomplishments with a big party.

# Chapter Twenty-Two: Making Tough Decisions

A foreign student had to maintain a minimum of a 2.5 grade point average in the academic classes. My average was not high enough to attend a state college or university. I was rejected admission because my average was 2.4, a little above average. One of the counselors suggested that I enroll in extension classes at UCLA for a year to raise my average and transfer to the state college. I took the counselor's advice and enrolled at UCLA.

To my surprise, I found UCLA to be invigorating and not as difficult as Glendale College. The students acted maturely in class, and the topics of discussions were sophisticated. The psychology professor raised our curiosity about human behavior, specifically our own. The further I delved into the subject, the more interested I became about human behavior. During my two semesters at UCLA, I enrolled in clinical psychology classes. I maintained a 3.5 grade point average. In the summer of 1969 was admitted to California State University, Los Angeles (CSULA) from where I graduated with a Bachelor of Arts degree in psychology in 1970.

CSULA is a commuter school. Almost all of the students were from working-class families. The students themselves worked part- or full-time and commuted to the campus. I continued working my flexible hours at Hudson and spent the rest of my waking hours on campus. This was during the height of the antiwar movement. On any given day, there were rallies against war, racism, and poverty. My feelings about racism and the pointless war in Vietnam compelled me to become an active participant in these rallies and demonstrations.

I joined the Black Students Union (BSU) to collectively fight for the rights of people of color and against the injustices perpetrated against minority students on campus. There were very few students of color at CSULA at that time. The black and Latino students had to link forces to have their voices heard. I joined both groups. Because of financial hardships, the minority students were dropping out of school and were being drafted and sent to Vietnam. Some of my colleagues who were drafted opted to either flee to Canada or, if lucky, joined the VISTA program, Volunteers in Service to America.

As the war intensified, so did the peace demonstrations. CSULA, UCLA, and USC selected a day for massive demonstrations. The organizers wanted to send yet another message to President Nixon to end the war and senseless killings. I was afraid that if the war persisted, Garcie would be reassigned to Vietnam. On the day of the demonstration, approximately 70 percent of the students walked out of their classes, marched, and sat on the San Bernardino Freeway. The media was out in full force to report every move of the participants. The demonstration was peaceful, and the message was loud and clear.

During most of the antiwar rallies, we were informed about the presence of undercover Secret Service and FBI agents. These agents sometimes infiltrated the leadership of the organizing groups to gather information about individuals. I was naïve about the workings of the intelligence-gathering agencies.

In the middle of one of the demonstrations, a colleague of mine yelled at me to disappear because the "narcs" were taking pictures. He was afraid that if they had a photograph of me and discovered that I was a foreign student they would deport me instantly. In my zeal to bring an end to the war, I never thought about what would happen to me if I was arrested or identified as one of the "troublemakers."

The massive nationwide demonstrations resulted in the war finally ending in 1972 and our troops being brought home. However, over 55,000 American lives were lost and countless young men injured. The war had divided the citizens into doves and hawks. Nonetheless, the time had come to forget the differences and engage in a healing process.

Veterans returning home were scoffed at and even denigrated instead of being hailed as heroes. Certain Americans who were against the war misdirected their feelings. They blamed the servicemen who were simply performing their duties for the atrocities rather than holding the president and the "war mongers" in Washington DC responsible.

I was a chameleon who joined various ethnic groups and participated in their activities. In the middle of a heated discussion about racism at a Black Students Union meeting, a member looked at me and said, "You aren't black and don't know what you are talking about. You live with the white folks in Glendale; you don't know anything about being like us."

At first, I was shocked at the comment, then immediately responded, "Well, I am on the inside fighting it out, while you are standing on the outside throwing stones."

I considered myself a person of color and thusly fought for equal rights for everyone. It was becoming apparent that although I was a minority, I was not the "right minority." I was emphatically reminded in Glendale that I was not white by the words and actions of some of the people. To be scorned by those whom I considered to be my comrades was beyond comprehension. Perhaps I was trying too hard to identify with a racial or ethnic group rather than being myself. After all, the African Americans did suffer tremendously from the time they were brought to the United

States as slaves. My fellow BSU member may have had a point in saying that I really could not fathom the plight of the black folks in America.

I did not attend another BSU or any other organization meeting. Instead, I devoted my time to my studies and working two jobs. The tuition at CSULA was $25 a unit. I needed to earn extra money in order to keep up with all the expenses. In between work and school, I managed to find time to party and spend some time at the beach.

# Chapter Twenty-Three: A Family and Career Man?

My correspondence with the family had diminished considerably. Whereas, in the beginning, I was writing a letter every other day, now I wrote once a month or even less. A letter from home asked if I could bring my sixteen-year-old brother Ashok to attend school in the United States. I knew that eventually I would have to fulfill my duty of bringing over family members who wanted to migrate.

Considering that I was not a citizen, I could not sponsor anyone. I spoke to Len about the request from the family. He said he would be happy to sponsor my brother. We acquired the necessary paperwork and sent them to the United States Immigration Office. The American Consulate in Fiji already had a file on Len, thus making the process of the sponsorship uncomplicated.

While the family in Fiji was waiting for Ashok's visa, I was informed by one of my lady friends that she was pregnant. This information sent me into shock. How could I be so careless and stupid? What was I going to do? For two days, I sat on the beach wondering what to do. Finally, I spoke to Len about my predicament. He did not lecture me about being irresponsible or that I had ruined my life, but spoke to me about the responsibility of having a family. As usual, Len was very logical and assured me that he would support me in whatever decision I made.

Ashok arrived from Fiji during the summer of 1970. We enrolled him in Glendale High School. I found my role changing from a carefree bachelor to that of an older brother and father. Although I felt responsible, Len was always there to take care of any needs that arose. The mere fact that Ashok had me to guide him in the new land made his transition into the American way of life easy. In addition, the overall climate of the country had changed since I first set foot on the soil. President Johnson had signed the Civil Rights Bill in 1964 prohibiting any kind of overt prejudice, and the immigration laws had been relaxed. Some Latinos and other foreigners moved into Glendale. Racism was still prevalent, but it was not as practiced overtly as in the years past.

I continued my studies in psychology at CSULA and increased my working hours at Hudson. My goal was to graduate with a Bachelor of Arts degree by the end of the year. On November 29, 1970, Chandra gave birth to a beautiful boy. We named the boy Dhyan De Caux Lal. Len was honored to have his grandson carry his name. Ashok moved out of the bedroom that we shared to make room for the baby. His sleeping on the couch did not last long because Len had given the tenants who lived in the middle house a notice to vacate so we could move in. Within two weeks, we moved into the house, got married, and launched a new life.

My new role as family man was so sudden that it took me a little while to realize that I had two extra lives to take care of. Armed with a bachelor's degree, I commenced my search for full-time employment. I secured a job as a claims examiner with Equitable Life Insurance Company. Short hair, a clean shave, and button-down shirts and ties replaced the long hair, beard, and island shirts. No longer was I the "island boy," but an average working American with a white-collar job.

The position was challenging at the beginning, but after I learned the routines, it became mundane. I realized that I was the only dark face in a sea of approximately one hundred white faces. My employment was based on my qualifications and the fact that the businesses needed to employ minorities to comply with the federal law mandating equal employment opportunities for all. I did not encounter any hostility or prejudice from my fellow workers.

Around six months into the position, boredom set in. I hated wearing the shirt and tie and playing the "business man" role. However, this was a well-paying job that offered promises for rapid advancement. To escape the boring routine, I volunteered to coach soccer at Glendale High School. Working with the high-school students and teaching them the fundamentals of playing the game was the highlight of my day.

At work, I often found myself daydreaming about being on the field and participating with the students in the daily practices. In addition to the interaction with the students, I enjoyed the association with the adults on campus, most of whom were my former teachers. I wondered how it would feel to be a teacher.

Following the yearly review of my performance, the manager recommended me for a pay raise and possibility for future advancement. I was elated by the evaluation result and for a brief moment thought about my career with the company and future monetary gains.

Len never did like the idea of me working for the sole purpose of making money. He had given up his scholarship at Oxford University in England and migrated to America, where he joined the union movement to help organize the workers. He had hoped that I would follow his example. Len was benevolent and unselfish. He wanted me to have a comfortable life but also help those who were less fortunate.

One day, I walked into the office of the district manager and asked for a moment of his time. I initiated our conversation by thanking him for employing me, providing me with assistance, and recommending me for advancement. He replied that everyone was pleased with my performance and assured me that I had a great future with the company. With great trepidation, I informed him that I was thinking about going back to school and wanted to resign within a month. He was astonished but asked me to submit a formal letter of resignation.

A week following my departure from Equitable, I enrolled in the masters program at CSULA. My intention was to receive a degree in psychology with a minor in special education. However, after doing volunteer work at a school for handicapped students, I became interested in working with the disabled. Therefore, when it came time for me to take the comprehensive exams, I took them in special education instead of psychology. In September of 1972, I was assigned to student teach for one semester in psychology at Marshall High School and the second semester at Carver Junior High School in South Central Los Angeles.

Students in good academic standing usually enrolled in the psychology classes in the high schools. I was assigned to teach two psychology classes at Marshall. Mr. Gerald Winesberg, a dynamic educator, was my master teacher. He consistently challenged the students to conduct research and look at the alternatives before making decisions. He used the Socratic method of teaching, questioning students and asking them to give a reason for their answers.

I followed Mr. Winesberg's example when it was my turn to conduct the lessons. Because the students were gifted, I challenged them to read the books pertaining to psychology that I had read as an undergraduate. My students were brilliant; they far exceeded my expectations. Class discussions and the quality of their research papers rivaled that of some of my college classes.

My association with Marshall High School reached beyond the classes I taught. During the breaks, I helped the administration with supervision.

While walking around, I stopped and spoke with students about how they liked school, sports, their personal lives, and any other subject in which they wanted to engage. Upon Mr. Winesberg's recommendation, I began holding rap sessions during lunch. Sometimes we had forty students bringing their lunch to the room to engage in discussions. Not only was I guiding the students, but I was learning from them as well. Sometimes, the vice principal, Jack Jacobson, sat in the back of the room and watched our noontime activity.

Mr. Jacobson asked if I had a moment because he wanted to speak with me. "Sure," I replied. He had a nice office with a leather chair and a big desk with papers piled in each corner. I thought that I had done something wrong and was going to be chastised by the vice principal. Instead, he began our conversation by saying, "Lal, I have been hearing about all the work you are doing with the students, and today I saw you in action. I am impressed with the way you communicate with the kids, especially the gang members. They open up to you and give you information that we have never been able to get. If you have time, I would like you to work in my office for a couple of hours helping me with discipline."

At first, Mr. Jacobson's comments and request bewildered me, but I quickly replied, "I would love to work in your office. It is such an honor for me. This is such a great opportunity for me to learn from you."

The next day, right after finishing my teaching, I reported to the office and was instantly assigned to speak with two students who had been in a fight. School rules clearly delineated that these students were to be suspended. My goal was to have the students realize their mistake, shake hands, and promise to refrain from any disruptive behaviors. I asked Mr. Jacobson's permission to bend the rule and not suspend the combatants. They were to remain after school and help the custodians clean the campus.

In my conversation with Jack Jacobson, I gave him the rationale for my decision. "I figured that if the students apologized to each other, recognized the foolishness of their actions, and were given an opportunity to select an alternative to suspension, they would accept the responsibility for their actions. I believe in 'positive discipline' rather than meting out punishment. The ultimate goal is to resolve the conflict and redirect the students' energy into a positive direction. Suspension is a temporary solution, but when the students return, the hostility and negative feelings remain with them, leading to the possibility of another conflict."

Jack Jacobson shook his head, saying, "You have a point there. I feel the same way, but it is difficult to convince a lot of people on this campus. They want immediate action, and suspension is the number one solution."

I became immersed in all aspects of the daily activities of Marshall. In early December, I suffered a severe appendicitis attack and was hospitalized for ten days. While in the hospital, I was visited by almost two-thirds of my students and several faculty members. I couldn't fulfill the required number of weeks in the teaching assignment to receive credit. CSULA officials informed me that I had to teach another four weeks at the high school the following semester or start all over again.

Jerry Winesberg and Jack Jacobson wrote letters to the university informing the dean of the School of Education about my involvement at Marshall and that the time I spent at the school far exceeded their requirements. They also met with the university supervisor and informed him that my performance in the assignment was above and beyond expectations. Based on the recommendations from the school and the supervisor, I was granted full credit for my student teaching assignment.

# Chapter Twenty-Four: Adventures in the Inner City

Upon completion of a month-long recuperation period, I was assigned to Carver Junior High School to fulfill the second tier of student teaching. Unlike Marshall High, where the students were primarily white and came from lower middle class to wealthy families, Carver's students were all black and from poor families. Ninety percent of the students were on the free federal meal program. The school and the neighborhood were plagued with gang violence. Student academic performance was extremely low and teacher turnover rates high. As many as one-third of the faculty members left the school at the end of each year.

My charge was to teach in a self-contained English class for the educable mentally retarded under the direction of Verneen Evans, a veteran teacher. She had been teaching at Carver for over twenty years and knew the older siblings, parents, and even grandparents of most of the students. Again, I was fortunate to have a skillful and dynamic master teacher. For the first week, I observed Verneen's classroom management style, dispatch activities, and the caring and compassionate manner in which she delivered instruction.

Every student that entered her class was greeted with a hug and a warm smile. Within a few days of observation, I discovered that a majority of the ninth-grade students academically functioned on the third-grade level or below. Some of the boys exhibited aggressive behaviors that caused Mrs. Evans to take them outside for a motherly talk. These students were not retarded; they had learning difficulties caused by varying degrees of emotional issues.

The most difficult part of teaching the class was obtaining and maintaining the attention of students. In the beginning, it was difficult for me to get the students to settle down so I could begin the lesson. They had short attention spans and constantly wanted to talk or walk around. Mrs. Evans had no problem gaining the students' attention and keeping them focused on specific tasks. She would stand in front of the class and simply look at them, and they would quiet down and take their seats. Through observing her and developing my own techniques, I sharpened my skills in classroom management and delivering instruction.

When students persisted on exhibiting negative behaviors, I spoke with them and visited their homes. Every time I went to one of the students' homes, they were surprised because rarely did anyone from the school venture out into the community due to safety concerns. Every day the principal or vice principal announced on the public address system, "It is now four o' clock. For your safety, anyone still on campus should leave immediately. All the gates will be locked in five minutes." I, on the other hand, would usually stay until five or six playing basketball with the students and other neighborhood youngsters.

Through the basketball games, I began to develop a rapport with the students. In one circumstance, a high-school student walked up to me and said, "Hey, we heard you're cool, man." He gave me his name and shook my hand. When I first saw this person walking toward me, I was a little scared. He had a swagger and a slight limp. This type of walk was known as "the Crip" walk. A majority of the students who identified with or romanced the gang lifestyle walked in this manner. While we were talking, a few of the students who were playing basketball or simply walking around gravitated toward us. They thought that there was going to be trouble, but once they came closer, they realized that we were having a friendly conversation. Some of my students yelled out my name, letting all the others know who I was.

Every day at Carver was a challenge because we did not know what kind of problem would arise—flooding in the bathroom, trash can on fire, fire alarm going off, or a gang fight. I received my baptism during lunch when a food fight broke out in the cafeteria. Mr. Purnell, the vice principal, asked me to assist him in diffusing the melee. As we ran inside, a milk carton came flying from across the room and hit me on the chest. I ran in the direction the milk carton came from and began grabbing students and telling them to leave the cafeteria. Within five minutes, the adults on supervision were able to disperse the students and bring the chaos under control.

Mr. Purnell thanked me for my help and apologized for the incident. The cafeteria was a total mess. Food was thrown on the ground and splattered against the wall, and some tables and chairs had been turned over. There I stood, drenched with milk and angry as hell. My first inclination was to leave the campus and never return. I wanted to teach and help these underprivileged kids, but their behavior appalled me. They showed a total disregard for anyone or anything.

Henry Purnell was a very hardworking man who spent long hours with the youngsters, even those who consistently challenged his authority. He was a proud black man who had "paid his dues" in the system and climbed through the ranks. He wanted the students to forsake the gang life and become members of the mainstream society. Henry spoke to students about the importance of education and the plight of the uneducated black person.

Unfortunately, very few of the students heeded his advice. All they knew was what they witnessed every day: an existence filled with poverty, violence, and drugs. The idea of going to college and becoming a professional was as remote as going to the moon for these youngsters.

Verneen Evans said she had heard about my experience in the cafeteria and advised me to be careful about jumping into a melee. She also let me know that she had received positive comments from students about my interaction with them after school. "They really like you. They say you're cool and don't treat them with disrespect." She further stated that she was pleased with my classroom management and teaching abilities. I was thrilled to hear such compliments from my master teacher because I was not sure about my instructional performance. Her positive comments gave me the impetus to work harder and spend more time with the students.

Two months into my teaching assignment, Mrs. Evans was asked to assume a part-time position as a counselor and specialist for the special education students. Since the school had difficulty acquiring substitute teachers, I was given the sole responsibility of the class under the supervision of Mrs. Evans. The university supervisor was reluctant, but agreed to the arrangement.

Being solely responsible for the class without having to rely on someone else for assistance forced me to try different strategies for teaching. I used the students' daily life experiences for my lessons and compared their immediate situations to incidences around the country and the world. My reality-based approach to disseminating information and holding "rap" sessions grabbed students' attention and increased their interest in learning.

I completed my student teaching assignment, was hired as a substitute teacher in March of 1973, and in August received a contract as a full-time teacher. During the summer, I attended CSULA to take classes toward the completion of my master's degree. While in school, I worked part-time with a federally funded program as a counselor for troubled youth. Working with the students enrolled in this program gave me further insight into the lives of inner-city black youth.

September 1973 was the beginning of my full-fledged career as an educator. I had a credential to teach and was given my own classroom and even a box in the main office with my name. As was customary, the school year began with a series of faculty meetings. Since I had already been at the school the previous year, I was not treated like a rookie, but was introduced as the new special education teacher. Classes were scheduled to begin in three days. I was ready with my lesson plans and materiel to fill the hungry minds with knowledge.

Well, I was in for a rude awakening. The first day brought with it new experiences of enrolling students, filling program cards, and other duties that created a chaotic atmosphere. I didn't know who was supposed to be in my class, how many students were misplaced, and which students were playing games to confuse the new teacher. No sooner had I entered my classroom than a fight broke out in front of my room. Students were running in all directions, pushing, kicking, and preventing the teachers from breaking up the fight. When the scene cleared, one student was taken to the nurse because he was bleeding profusely from his nose, and another with a torn shirt was escorted by the school security to Mr. Purnell's office.

Two combatants were apprehended, but others managed to escape. By the time I managed to usher my students into the classroom, half of the period was over. Once inside, the students continued to speak about the fight without any acknowledgment of my attempts to bring order. Finally, I picked up a chair and threw it against the wall. The students were stunned at my behavior. Suddenly, the room was quiet. "Now, there are two things that I do best, teach and kick ass. Which one do you want?" I screamed. I yelled at them to shut up and take their seats.

Someone muttered, "This nigger is crazier than we are."

The fact that I was about 215 pounds and had long hair and a beard gave me somewhat of a menacing appearance. Some students knew me from the previous year, but those who didn't, did not know what to make of my tirade. Then a slender student who was about my height quietly walked from the back of the room toward me, got in my face, and said, "You motha fucker, I'm going to fuck you up."

I was petrified and did not know how to respond. So I placed my hands on my face, pulled them down slowly, and retorted, "I told your mother not to tell anyone."

He was shocked at my response and did not know what to say. Some members of the class said, "Wooooo, he got you."

While the class was laughing and making noise, I asked this young man to come outside with me. He refused and asked why. "Just come with me," I demanded in a stern voice. Reluctantly, he followed me outside. As the door closed, all the students ran toward the door to peek from the little window to see what was going on. I pretended to yell and point my finger in the young man's face, but in reality I was saying, "Look, man, you seem like the leader of the class. I need your help in making sure everyone behaves. If everyone does what they are supposed to, you will get an A."

He stared at me as if I was crazy. "You're shittin' me."

"No," I said. "I know you are smart, so when we walk in, you take over the class and be my assistant."

Before we walked back in, I asked his name. "Tommy," he replied in a very cold and angry manner. When the students saw us turning to come in, they scurried back to their seats. I did not say a word when we entered the room. Tommy began, "Hey, man, why don't all of you quiet down and see what this dude has to say." The students looked at Tommy, then me, and slowly began to quiet down. One student persisted on talking and cursing. Tommy looked in his direction. "Boy, if you don't shut your mouth, I'm gonna kick your ass." I quickly explained to the class that Tommy was my assistant and that he was responsible for helping me in my daily teaching duties.

Henry Purnell and some of the teachers apprised me that Tommy was the leader of the Four-Tray Crip Gang. He was feared and respected by his peers in the community. Although Tommy was at school on most days, he was rarely present in his classes. Part of my bargain with him was that he attended my class every day. He was responsible for taking roll and making sure that all the other students were seated when the bell rang. My gamble with Tommy produced positive results. Because of his leadership, I had little or no classroom management problems, and even the destructive behaviors in the hallway decreased.

Each day, Tommy came to class with the other students following behind him. The students received grades for their behavior and academic performance daily. Tommy consistently received As in both areas. By helping others and sitting next to my desk, he began to read and learn to do math. He was interested in sports, so I asked him to bring the sports section of the *Los Angeles Times*, and we would read the articles in it. Before long, Tommy was reading about football players like Walter Payton, and for math, he was able to calculate the average gained by Payton during each game.

By calculating each player's statistics, it wasn't long before Tommy was comparing Walter Payton's net average yard per run to that of O. J. Simpson and other top runners. He was able to do the same for basketball and baseball players. Not bad for a kid who hated math and could barely do simple computations. Other students began to emulate Tommy. I found myself teaching English by using *Jet* magazine, auto magazines, and other materials that were of interest to students.

Dhyan Lal

In the ninth-grade class, about twelve of the students were going to be sixteen years old by summertime. Most of them wanted to learn how to drive, but they could not receive a learner's permit because of their inability to read. On my way home, I stopped by the California Department of Motor Vehicles (DMV) and picked up some driving handbooks.

For the entire second half of the school year, the students read, discussed, and took tests on the material contained in the handbook. I was surprised at the progress the students were making. Whereas, previously they could barely spell a simple word, now they were correctly spelling words such as *pedestrian* and *maximum*. In May of 1974, we went to the DMV to take the test. Nine out of the twelve students passed their test and were able to receive their learners' permits.

My involvement with the students continued outside of the classrooms. Some of the other teachers and I implemented an after-school athletic program where students engaged in sports competitions. The teams competed within their grade level, and the two teams with the best records played for the championship. Now, rather than engaging in gang activities, students spent time at school and expanded their energy by participating in organized sports. My homeroom class won the championship for both basketball and football in the ninth-grade category.

Travis Kiel, the dean of students, and I organized weekend events and field trips to keep the students occupied and show them that there was life outside of the ghetto. Travis was a tall black man who had played college basketball and had grown up in a similar environment. He was thrilled at my idea and suggested that we write a proposal to the district and some of the public institutions to secure funds for our endeavors. We were able to receive financial support from the Los Angeles Unified School District and some community-based organizations to begin our program. Students had to enroll in the weekend program and meet attendance and behavioral criteria to qualify to participate.

Our first trip was to the snow in the San Bernardino Mountains. Out of the 150 students who went on the trip, more than two-thirds had never seen or touched snow. I had come from a small island and within a few months had been able to take a trip to the snow. These children were born a short distance from the snow but had never seen it. Similarly, a large number of students had not been to the beach or an amusement park. Our program consisted of lessons about each place that we visited and discussions on what the students felt about their experiences.

A young man was shocked to see women clad in tiny bikinis lying in the sun on a visit to Malibu Beach. He remarked, "I thought they only did that in movies. Look at that white woman; she's naked."

Students were also marveled by the homes they saw in different locales. A girl looked at Travis and said, "Mr. Kiel, I want to grow up and live in a house like this one in a place like this."

Introducing the young people to the world beyond poverty and despair helped improve their academic and social behavior. Conversations about the importance of education seemed to be getting through to some of the students. I can't say that we experienced tremendous success overnight, but by going the extra mile, we were able to touch and save a number of lives. We did have some disappointments, including my favorite Tommy, who was arrested in high school for aggravated assault and sent to juvenile hall.

I spent four very challenging but gratifying years at Carver. The poverty and despair that I witnessed made me wonder about the class and race culture of America. After all, this was the land of plenty where the streets were supposedly paved with gold. At least that's what the people in Fiji thought. I had discovered a somewhat different America.

Although only a few miles apart, the people of Glendale and those in South Los Angeles lived entirely different lives. For all practical purposes, these were two different countries. I had studied American history and

Dhyan Lal

learned about slavery, prejudice, and the Civil War. Nevertheless, things were supposed to have changed in the twentieth century. Somehow, equality for all had come to mean separate and unequal, despite the passage of the 1964 Civil Rights Bill.

# Chapter Twenty-Five: The Lal Family's Pilgrimage

Despite what I knew and shared with the family back home about the hardships faced by the poor and people of color in America, their perceptions did not change. They all wanted to come and enjoy the comforts of this modern society. One by one, I sponsored family members who wanted to migrate. First it was Babu; then my oldest brother, Gautam, and his family; my sister Lalli and her family; and later, in 1981, my sister Gal and her family, along with my mother and father. My father did not want to leave the comforts of the Islands, but relented to the pressure from the rest of the family. He was a proud man who had built his own house, knew everyone in the community, and did not want to start all over in a foreign land.

As family members arrived, it was my duty to help them acclimate and settle in the new country. Len was gracious enough to open his home to all the relatives. By 1975, 800 East Windsor Road had become little Fiji. The idea of the family slowly getting together again delighted Len. He had continuously questioned himself about the prudence of taking me away from a happy family when I was only thirteen years old. Now he felt that bhai and he had made a good decision. I had lived up to their expectations by receiving a good education and had become the conduit for others to realize their dreams.

Living together in the two houses that were right next to each other with a small grassy area separating them created a village-like atmosphere. Again, we were a big happy family with Len being the chief. Since Len's daughter, Shirley, her husband, and four children moved to Texas, we were the only family he had. He relished sitting on the porch reading while the children played outside. When it was just Len and I, we cooked and cleaned for ourselves. Now Len was served three meals a day and did not have to worry about having to clean the dishes or the house.

Ever since my arrival in the United States, I looked forward to the day when the entire family could be together. Well, the family was slowly getting together, but there was something missing. I did not feel that I was as close to the family as they were to each other. At first, I thought it was me, but before long, my feelings were affirmed. On numerous occasions, the family gathered at a park for a picnic or went on outings and did not inform or invite me. When I asked them, they replied that they did not think I was interested. For the first time, I realized that my absence had created a distance in our relationship. They looked upon me as the "American" who would not enjoy these gatherings.

Eventually, the family outgrew the living arrangement in Glendale. There were too many of us for the limited space. About a year earlier, Babu and his wife had moved to Venice, California, to be close to his wife's relatives. I bought a house in Sunland, in the hills above Glendale. Gautam moved into the house that I formerly occupied, and my sister and her family stayed with Len. Ashok, who was on a foreign student visa, had stopped going to school and started working full-time. He was advised by the immigration department to either go back to school or face deportation. Rather than face deportation, he moved to Canada for a while and then back to Fiji.

It was rather strange; no sooner had the family reunited and lived as if they were in the Islands than they began to go their separate ways. What I failed to realize was that these were not the same people whom I had left in 1962 or visited in 1966. My brothers and sisters were now grown men and women with their own families. They wanted to have their own homes, cars, and all the other amenities. I guess my memory was fixated in a period where everything remained the same.

Working full-time, going to school, and taking care of my immediate and extended family was difficult, to say the least. The constant demands for assistance from family members and visits by extended family from Fiji took its toll on my personal life. Chandra let me know that she could not take care of everyone else and wanted her own space. I had a feeling that since I was spending so much time with my relatives, she was feeling rejected. Actually, she was jealous. No matter where I went, I always made sure that my son, Dhyan, whom we nicknamed Gogi because of his devilish behavior, was with me. Chandra rarely wanted to take part in family gatherings, opting to go and visit her own family in Venice.

Despite the trouble brewing in my personal relationship, I continued helping others and pursuing a second master's degree in school administration. One evening when I returned from work, Chandra informed me that she had spoken with her family and they agreed that we should go our own separate ways. I knew that sooner or later we would be having this discussion. She was young, twenty-two years old. The responsibility that I had placed on her was even too much for an older person. I concurred with her decision and said that she could take all the materialistic possessions, but could not take Gogi. No way was I going to part with my son.

Gogi was five years old and attending a kindergarten school in Glendale. On most days, I would take him to school on my way to work and pick him up on my way back. So I told Chandra that her family could come the next day and move her. That evening, when I opened the door to the house, Gogi looked at me and said, "Daddy, we have been robbed; everything is gone." He ran into his room to see if his bed and toys had also gone. Much to his delight, his room was left untouched. He looked into our bedroom and found it empty. "Your bed is gone too. Where are you and Mom going to sleep? Where is Mom?" I explained to him that his mother had gone away for a while and that he and I were going to stay in the house. "Where will you sleep?" he asked.

"I will camp in your room," I replied. He liked that idea.

The next day after work, I picked Gogi up from school and went to visit Len. As soon as we entered the house, Gogi ran up to Len, yelling, "Unkie."

Len picked him up, saying, "Hey, there's my boy." The look in his eyes and the joy he expressed were clear indications of Len's love for his grandson.

As always, the first thing Gogi asked was, "Do you have any candy?"

"Of course," said Len. "Let's go to the room and get some."

Len always kept candy in his desk drawer. All the neighborhood children knew exactly where the candy was kept, and upon entering the house, they usually headed for the desk. I told him that I had something very important to talk with him about and asked him to go to dinner with us. During dinner, I apprised him of my situation. At first, he was dismayed and upset, but later he responded, "I only have one question: What about Gogi?"

"I am keeping him," I replied.

Len's caring ways and logical characteristic made me feel comfortable about discussing my problems. He asked me about my plans for the future. I informed him that I was going to stay in the house for the time being and concentrate on pulling my life back together. "I never had to worry about you; you always were very calculating and knew what you wanted," he said while placing his hand on mine. He had brought me up to think about the impact my actions would have on others before making decisions. Rather than giving me a lecture, he simply stated, "If you need anything, just ask." The response I received from Len was exactly what I expected. His words of solace were filled with encouragement. I was very lucky to have someone like Len, who was not only a father, but also a friend.

For the next few months, I spent a majority of my time working, going to school, and taking care of Gogi. While I was attempting to enroll in a class that was overcrowded, a young lady approached me and asked if she could take my place on the waiting list because she really needed the class. I said that I also needed the class, but not to worry since all of us would probably gain entrance. She gave me a stern look and sat down.

When the professor was finished, he stated that he could take the first five people on the waiting list. After class, I introduced myself to my classmate. She was still angry, but told me that her name was Shirley and that she was a consultant in the deaf and hard of hearing program with Los Angeles Unified School District.

Through our conversations in and out of class, we discovered that both of us had received our master's degree in special education and were working with handicapped children, she with deaf children and I with the mentally retarded. As fate would have it, both of us were now taking classes to receive an administrative credential to pursue our goals of entering school administration.

We began to study together, and before the school term was over, we started seeing each other socially. Our professional and personal friendship flourished over the next three months.

My family from Fiji was embarking on a new life in the new land. In a similar fashion, I was also setting sail on a new beginning. In March of 1976, Shirley and I decided to move in together in a rented house in

Sunland. The house was located on a quiet street and had a nice backyard for the boys, Boogie and Gogi, to play. Every morning, we drove the boys to school on our way to work and picked them up on our way back. Whenever Len came to visit, he spoiled the boys by buying them whatever they wanted. They would also talk him into taking them to the fast-food restaurants, something that we never did.

Lalli, my eldest sister, her husband, and the two boys visited us often. She intimated that they would like to live close to us, but they did not have enough money to move out of Len's house. Lucky for them, one Saturday while my youngest sister, Girly, and her husband, James, were visiting from Fiji, we saw a three-bedroom house for sale. The house was empty, and there was an open-house sign in front. Walking through the house and speaking with the real-estate agent, we discovered that the owners were anxious to sell and would entertain any reasonable offer. Girly and James liked the house and thought Lalli and Ramesh would like it very much. Without any further discussion, we made an offer on the house.

Much to our surprise, the agent telephoned the owners, who verbally accepted the offer. James and Girly signed the offer papers. The next day, we brought Ramesh and Lalli to see the house; they fell in love with it and wished that they could afford to buy it. Shirley and I said, "Well, if you like it, then it's yours."

They were perplexed by our statement and looked in the direction of Girly and James. Girly smiled and said, "They bought this house for you yesterday when we were riding around. We signed your names and the agent is going to complete the forms today." With tears in her eyes, Lalli hugged us, saying, "Thank you," while still in disbelief.

All of our lives were changing at a rapid pace. I was very pleased to have Lalli and Ramesh living close to us. The boys now had two cousins to play with. Len was a little disappointed to see them leave Glendale. Nevertheless, he realized that they would move into their own place eventually. Now when he came up on weekends, he had two families to visit with and four little boys to spoil. Meanwhile, Gautam remained in Glendale, living next door to Len in the house I previously occupied. All the adults in the family had found jobs and were providing for their families.

In June, we decide to take a trip to Fiji for Ashok's wedding and to spend the entire summer recapturing the easy life. As we didn't want to pay rent for three months, we placed all our belongings in storage and departed for our journey to the South Pacific. On our way to Fiji, we stopped in American Samoa for four days.

Our plane landed in Pago Pago at four in the morning. It was so hot and muggy that on the way to the hotel, the taxi driver had to run his wipers as if it was raining. Our hotel was located on the beach with the back sliding doors opening onto a cove that had beautiful white sand and pristine blue water. After a brief nap, the boys were up and into the water with their underwear on. Shirley and I were not far behind; we quickly put on our bathing clothes and jumped into the water right behind the boys.

Boogie and Gogi were surprised to find how warm the water was. In Los Angeles, the ocean is cold, causing bathers to get out of the water in a short time. We must have played and swam for quite a while until the boys reminded us that we hadn't eaten all day. They were hungry, but it was a tough decision to eat or stay in the water, especially since they befriended a little boy riding in a little tin canoe. The Samoan boy was about seven, with the courage of an adult. He maneuvered his homemade canoe like an expert. They were mesmerized by his skills and asked if they could join him. Being the island boy, I said they could climb in, but Shirley didn't feel very comfortable about letting them get into the tiny canoe.

Walking around Pago Pago, eating fresh food, and conversing with the locals made us feel right at home. It wasn't long before half the island knew that a family from Fiji was staying in the hotel where only the *palagi*, the white people, resided. Because we were considered locals, we received the local price at the restaurants, markets, and in all our purchases.

While buying some souvenirs at a store, I inadvertently left my camera. About two hours later, I realized that I had lost the camera. Retracing our steps, we came back to the store to find that the lady behind the counter had found it and was waiting for us to come back. Shirley's family was from Trinidad and British Guyana, so she understood the island culture, yet the reception we received in Samoa made a lasting impression on her.

Before we realized it, it was time to pack the belongings and catch the plane to Fiji. Before boarding the airplane, I glanced at the arrival section of the tiny thatched hut airport terminal and saw Gyan, his wife, and three-year-old son, Niraj. I yelled out his name. He was astonished and turned his head to see who was calling him in this remote place. He saw me waving.

Leaning over the barricade, I inquired, "What are you doing here?"

"By stopping here, we saved money," he replied. The downside to this venture was that planes only came into Samoa every four days. We had befriended the ground hostess who was born and raised in Fiji. I asked her if Gyan and his family could join us. As luck would have it, the generous hostess allowed them to join us instead of having to wait the mandatory four days for another flight.

I had not seen Gyan during the time I was getting my life together. Neither one of us knew about the other going back home. Amma, bhai, Girly, and James were surprised to see us step out when the taxi pulled in front of the house. It was Saturday afternoon, and as expected, there were about five or six people sitting on a mat in the front yard playing cards and drinking kava. I hadn't been home in ten years, and this was the first visit for Shirley and the boys. Walking toward the font door brought back memories of childhood.

Boogie and Gogi could not wait to change their clothes and join their cousins in chasing the chickens around the yard. It took them all of one minute to become acclimated to the surroundings and take advantage of the open fields. They climbed the guava tree by the side of the house and picked some ripe guavas. Then they chased a big red rooster into the bushes. The rooster, along with the fresh fish James had bought from a fisherman by the river, was our main course for dinner.

Meeting Gyan in Pago Pago was fortunate since he was well known around the island and was invited to a different place every night for dinner. Having left Fiji fourteen years ago, I was treated more like a visitor than a local. Regardless, almost every day we were inundated with requests to go for lunch or dinner. The boys especially enjoyed visiting family and friends who lived along the beach or in the countryside. Once, while we were swimming, Boogie screamed as if he had been bitten by something. I rapidly swam to him only to find that the string from his swimming trunks was hanging, and the fish were attempting to bite it.

We borrowed James's car and explored the big island of Viti Levu. This was my first attempt at driving on the left-hand side and on the gravel roads. Initially, I was a bit apprehensive, but after an hour or so, I became accustomed to driving on the wrong side and negotiating the turns on the rough winding roads. Throughout the journey, we were treated to breathtaking mountain and ocean views, lush green forests, and wide-open spaces.

The narrow roads barely had enough room for one car to travel. On one occasion, I was lost and looked for a place to turn around with no success. Shirley and the boys were afraid and kept urging me to find a place quickly. I saw a slight clearing and made an attempt to turn the car. Just as I was turning, four teenagers with their faces painted and carrying spears jumped out of the bushes. They stood by the side of the road staring at us. Needless to say, everyone was terrified at the sight. I waved at the fearless warriors without receiving any response. They stood very still, just as surprised to see us as we were to see them. I hastily turned around the car and headed back to the main road. The boys were on the verge of tears, and Shirley had a ghostly look on her face.

I had always heard people say, "Time flies when you're having fun." Well, this statement was never truer than it was during our visit. Time appeared to have flown so quickly that three months seemed like three weeks. It was already the beginning of September and time for us to return. None of us was ready to leave the carefree, relaxing, and peaceful lifestyle.

We reluctantly packed our bags and prepared to leave our island home. A remorseful feeling permeated throughout the house. We had become such an important part of the family that our pending departure would create a void. Bhai, who rarely showed any emotion, had grown attached to Boogie and Gogi. Even he exhibited signs of sadness.

At the Nadi airport, the crying, hugging, and saying goodbye for the umpteenth time made our departure more difficult. One is never certain when, if ever, he will again see the people he is leaving behind. This uncertainty fueled the anguish and further caused tears to flow freely. However, it was time to leave paradise behind and head back to reality.

# Chapter Twenty-Six: Facing the Challenges of Racism

Returning to Los Angeles was a culture shock. We had spent three months in a place where life was simple and time was of no essence. Now we were "back to the future." People at the airport were rushing, the cars were honking, and the traffic was at a standstill. I glanced at Shirley and rhetorically asked, "Why did we ever come back?" Lalli and Ramesh were anxiously waiting for our arrival. They wanted to hear all the news from home.

On the ride back, the boys could not talk enough about their adventures. "You guys sound like you wanted to stay in Fiji," Lalli said.

"We wanted to stay longer and play," the boys replied.

We were back, but with no place to stay. For the next two months, we lodged at Lalli's. In the meantime, we searched for a house to purchase. A few weeks of concerted efforts resulted in us finding a beautiful three-bedroom house with a big kitchen, living room, and swimming pool on a quiet street half a mile from Lalli and Ramesh. The boys were thrilled at the prospect of having a place with a nice backyard and a pool. So, in November of 1976, we moved into our new home.

Although we had comfortably settled in our home, driving to our jobs in Los Angeles and going to school at night was taking its toll on us. In order not to leave the boys at the babysitter's for extended periods of time, we took turns taking classes. For example, if Shirley's classes convened on Mondays and Wednesdays, then I enrolled in classes on Tuesdays and Thursdays. At no time did we want the family to suffer from neglect. There were times, however, when we did have to leave the boys with the babysitter for longer than we cared to.

We enrolled Gogi in the first grade and Amrit (Boogie) in kindergarten at Sunland Elementary School. Sunland Elementary was a small neighborhood school comprised of small buildings surrounded by trees. The boys promptly became involved in the extracurricular and sport activities of the school.

Being gregarious, the boys had no trouble making friends. Before long, we were having weekend pool parties for their friends with Mommy and Daddy assigned to the barbeque duties. Daddy was also acting as lifeguard and swim teacher. My swimming lessons were designed after kaka's two-step method. A number of neighborhood boys and girls learned how to swim very quickly through this technique.

Conversations regarding school and the day's events were the norm at the dinner table. Whenever the boys were asked, "How was school today, and what did you do?" their response was always the same: "Fine." Despite their reluctance to engage in conversations about their schoolwork, we asked specific questions to elicit responses.

One day, both of the boys became angry about our usual inquiry about school and responded in a manner that was totally out of character. Boogie mumbled, "I hate this school."

"Why?" Shirley asked.

"Because the kids are mean, and they bother us."

After speaking with two of their best friends, Mike and Sherry Wells, we discovered that some of the boys in school had been calling Boogie and Gogi names such as "greasers," "niggers," "wetbacks," etc. We also found out that gangs of boys were attempting to beat our kids, and Mike and Sherry came to their rescue. Hearing about the racism our boys were encountering made my blood boil. We had moved into a nice home in a neighborhood that we thought was ideal to raise a family in only to find that one cannot judge a book by its cover.

We asked the boys to disregard the comments made by these ignorant people. "Yeah, but those American kids hide and wait for us after school. They chase us, and if they catch us, they try to beat us," Boogie responded.

I said, "Look, if they start a fight, do not run; make sure that you get in your fair share of punches."

Gogi was quiet for a while then looked at Boogie and said, "We got two of them in the bathroom yesterday."

"What happened?" Shirley asked.

"I was going to the bathroom and saw two of the boys who had beat us up the other day. So I went to Boogie's class and signaled to him; he got a pass to the bathroom, and we went in there and fought with those guys."

Like a typical father, I asked, "Who won?"

"We did," responded the boys with smiles on their faces. "Those guys ran out of there crying."

I knew that Sunland was an all-white area populated by working-class people, but I did not expect six- and seven-year-olds to suffer the indignities that I had suffered in the early sixties in Glendale. This quiet little town in a country-like setting was far removed from the hustle and congestion of Los Angeles. The surrounding hills and Big Tujunga Canyon with a beautiful creek flowing through it enhanced the beauty of the area. What we did not know was that the community was settled by the Ku Klux Klan and other hate groups.

We advised the boys to inform their teachers about being called names and harassed to and from school. The boys responded, "These teachers hear the kids call us names and tell us to go back where we came from, but they don't do anything. When we tell them what happened on the playground, they tell us to go and play."

Listening to their comments brought back the horrid memories of my own experiences and how Garcie and I had to fight the battles against prejudice. Finally, I said, "From now on, if someone tries to hurt you on purpose, beat the hell out of them. If they are a gang, both of you protect each other."

A few days after our conversations with the boys, we received a phone call and a letter from the principal of Sunland Elementary asking us to come to the school for a conference concerning Dhyan and Amrit. We waited in the principal's office for a while before she came and greeted us. She was a middle-aged woman with blond hair and was impeccably dressed. After the introductions, she retrieved a piece of paper from her desk and began to read about a number of allegations made against the boys by other students and some teachers. Then she began to tell us about the kind of school she ran, and if the boys did not refrain from fighting, they would be "kicked out of school."

Without really saying the words, the principal intimated that because the boys were different, they were the cause of the problems. We patiently listened to the principal's diatribe without response until she stated, "I know it is difficult for people like you to understand, but they cannot behave like that in school."

When she was finished, Shirley and I simultaneously said, "What do you mean by people like us?"

"Now, you listen," Shirley emphatically responded. "Have you ever bothered to ask the boys why they fight? Do you know that gangs of boys have chased them on their way home from school? Do you know that the teachers ignore them when they complain about other kids calling them derogatory names? Before you talk about suspensions, you better get your facts straight."

When Shirley was finished, I stated, "I advised the boys to fight back and not stand there and let someone beat up on them. We have had enough of our kids being referred to with racial slurs without you or anyone else doing anything about it. And by the way, my wife is a consultant and I am a teacher with Los Angeles School District. We are fully aware of the responsibilities of school officials and the rights of parents. You can do whatever you want, but I will call the board of education and a friend, Assistant Superintendent Mr. Anton, to inform them about our conversation and your attitude toward our children."

All of a sudden, her entire demeanor changed. "Oh, you don't have to call anyone. We can solve the problem at school. Amrit and Dhyan are very good students. I will speak with them and find out who the kids are that are picking on them. As educators, you understand the large number of problems that occur on a campus and how difficult it is to stay on top of everything."

"Well, we want our boys to feel comfortable at this school and not develop negative feelings toward schooling and education," I replied.

The bigotry that the boys faced at school also raised its ugly head in the neighborhood. One evening after taking a shower, I put on my *sulu*, a wraparound with a tropical floral design, and sat down to watch Monday Night Football. All of a sudden, I heard thunderous noise coming from the front of the house. I jumped from the chair and raced to the front door. Opening the front door, I found several big rocks that had been thrown at the house. I immediately knew that this was an attempt to intimidate us into leaving the neighborhood. After telling Shirley about the source of the noise, I picked up my *sele, a Fijian cane knife that is used in the bushes, and sat close to the door.*

*About half an hour later, several rocks and beer bottles hit the door. I opened the door and saw a group of high-school-aged boys running up the street. Barefoot and in my sulu, I chased the culprits and caught one of them. I pulled him by his long blond hair and slammed him to the ground. "If you move, I'll chop your head off," I yelled, with the sele pointed to his neck.*

He began to cry and begged me not to kill him. "Tell me where the other boys ran to." He pointed at the house across the street. I sternly pulled him up by the hair and said, "If I ever see you by the house or heard that you were bothering someone, I will come looking for you." As soon as I released him, he ran further up the street, made a right turn, and disappeared.

I walked across the street to the house the boy had pointed out, banged on the door, and rang the doorbell. A man in his forties opened the door and asked, "What do you want?"

"Some kids who threw rocks and bottles at my house were seen running in here," I replied.

He was holding what appeared to be a gun in his right hand. "No one is in here but my son," he retorted.

"Your son was one of the kids who threw the rocks."

He moved the gun around in his hand. I stared at his hand and said, "Go ahead use that, but before you can raise that hand, I will chop it off.

"I came here to tell your son and his friends to stop throwing rocks at my house and yelling racial slurs. If they don't stop, I will take matters into my own hands."

The man glared at me for a while, looked at my sulu, and finally said, "Okay, goodbye," slamming the door. From then on, I would put on my sulu, sit on the front porch, and read the paper while the boys played.

Neighbors would wave as they drove by or stop by to chat. The word about the rock-throwing incident and my response had spread through the neighborhood like a wild fire. Some people dropped by to apologize for the behavior of the delinquents and to inquire about our country of origin. I was always happy to let the people know about my island heritage and that we were not going to allow anyone to drive us out.

A few months later, a young Puerto Rican family moved into the house across the street. Like us, they were both professionals, working as executives in the banking industry. They had a boy about eight years old who befriended Boogie and Gogi. For the first few months, we waved at our new neighbors without engaging in any lengthy conversations. However, one evening, Maynord came to the door, introduced himself, and invited us to a community meeting at his house the following night. He explained that their house had been robbed. His wife, Norma, had lost some expensive jewelry and family heirlooms. Additionally, "Go back where you came from" was written on the living room wall.

The meeting at Maynord's was sparsely attended. A local police officer spoke about safety and how to establish a neighborhood watch. Following the meeting, when everyone had left, Shirley and I shared our experiences with Maynord and Norma. At the end of our conversation, which lasted until midnight, we concluded that we would watch out for each other. We had two factors common: one, that we were the only non-whites, and two, that we both had purchased the best homes in the area.

The epitaphs written on Maynord and Norma's wall and the ones verbally hurled at us earlier were motivated by ignorance and jealousy. Some residents took exception to the fact that foreigners like us could move into the neighborhood and buy the premium homes.

It did not take long for the Lals and Keysors to become the best of friends. We had pool parties, celebrated holidays together, and often dined at each other's homes. Little by little, we became accepted into the community. Friends of little Maynord and Boogie and Gogi's came to swim at both of our homes. The boys joined Little League baseball, and I became the manager of their team. Maynie was assigned to another team, thus setting up a friendly rivalry. Sports has a way of easing racial tensions. We made new friends, and I even met an old friend from high school, Tony Piscitelli, whose son was assigned to my team.

Still, not everything was always at ease. For instance, during one of my speeches to the team about the need to work hard, practice, and support the teammates, a parent yelled to his son, "You don't have to listen to that foreigner. Just go out there and play." I took an exception to the comment and told the parent that if he didn't like what I was doing, he could take his son off of my team.

Tony was very upset and replied, "One more comment out of you, and I'm going to kick ass." Later, several of the parents apologized for the rude comments of the one individual.

In September of 1978, our beautiful daughter, Roshni, was born. Instantly, she became the favorite of all our family and friends. The boys were ecstatic about having a little sister. Shirley obtained a year's leave from her job and stayed home to take care of the baby. In the meantime, we decided to add a second story to our home with two bedrooms and a bathroom. With Mommy home to take care of the children, I began teaching college four nights a week. I also transferred from Carver to Sun Valley Junior High School, seven miles down the hill from the house.

We became active members of the Sunland community. The boys joined the school band and performed at numerous concerts. Roshni was growing up rapidly, and before we knew it, she was in preschool. Boogie and Gogi graduated with honors from Sunland Elementary and Mount Gleason Junior High School. In fact, Gogi was elected the student body president at Mount Gleason. The academic and athletic abilities of Boogie and Gogi made them the most popular students on campus and in the community. One more time, the Lal family had overcome adversities and persevered.

# Chapter Twenty-Seven: Education Is a Way of Life, Not Just a Job

Moving to Sun Valley Junior High School cut my commute tremendously, but it brought with it some new challenges. I changed schools under a program in Los Angeles Unified School District that granted permission for minority teachers to transfer to schools that had a predominantly white faculty and staff. When I arrived at Sun Valley, I was only one of five minority teachers out of seventy-five. The other three special education teachers seized the opportunity to place the most difficult and severely emotionally disturbed students in my class. I was assigned a self-contained eighth grade class of fourteen boys. On the first day, a student from the back of the room hollered to his friend, "Hey, look, we got a nigger for a teacher."

I raised my head and without asking who had said that, I simply stated, "Then you must be in the wrong class, because my name is Mr. Lal."

My comment briefly quieted the students. I pulled my chair to the middle of the room and asked them to place their chairs in a circle for a discussion. I began the conversation by telling the students about where I grew up, how I came to America, and the path that led me into the teaching profession. The students were interested in my story, had numerous questions about Fiji, and gradually took turns talking about their own lives.

Despite the interruptions due to outbursts of behaviors on the part of some of the class members, we were able to learn a great deal about each other. Sharing experiences, likes, and dislikes enabled the students to find out more about their colleagues and themselves.

I had a big classroom that allowed me to create learning centers. For science, we set up an aquarium and a terrarium, and placed microscopes in one corner. For math, we built a mock store out of cardboard and brought in empty cans and boxes to put on the shelves and a couple of cash registers. The building and upkeep of all centers was the responsibility of the students.

I believe that if the students have the opportunity to have input and are given the responsibility and ownership for their learning, they will perform with interest and zeal. A parent donated a couch and an easy chair for our library and reading center. The reading center was stocked with materials requested by the students. They looked forward to sitting on the couch and reading their favorite magazines upon completion of the required assignments.

If the students exhibited exemplary behaviors during the week, I rewarded them by cooking tacos, hamburgers, and other food items on Fridays. The cooking sessions became a big hit. I used the purchasing of food items as a math lesson comparing prices and quantity. Before long, counselors and administrators were joining us for lunch.

Many of the teachers and counselors could not believe that these handicapped students were not only achieving academically and socially, but were speaking fondly of their class and the school. Additionally, the students were rewarded with field trips to parks, tide pools, auto plants, banks, and other places to widen their horizons. Because of my success in the classroom, the principal asked me to be a part-time counselor during the afternoons, an assignment I gladly accepted.

Some of the projects in which the students engaged kept us at school until five or six in the afternoon. We also spent some Saturdays on campus working in the vegetable garden. Older siblings and parents of the students as well as my own family became involved with the class. Before I knew it, the school year came to an end. I accepted the assignment to teach a summer school class, which primarily consisted of my students from the previous year. Usually summer school special education classes were tough, but I had the best of both worlds: a summer job and my own students. As a reward to the students, I made a deal with the local public swimming pool to take the students swimming every Friday for the six-week summer school session.

A week before the new school year began, Shirley, the boys, and I went to my room and prepared it for the opening day. When some of my students saw us working, they joined us. Unlike my first year, the opening day of school was very smooth. I was lucky because I inherited the same students who were now in the ninth grade and somewhat more mature.

The parents of these students and I had established relationships—so much so that I had visited the home of every child at one time or another and even dined with several families. At one of the homes, a mother said, "I don't know what you are doing, but James says that you are a better cook than me; he really likes your spaghetti."

I laughed and replied, "All the students help in the cooking session on Fridays, so the credit goes to all of them."

I began to apply for other positions. In October of 1978, I was interviewed for the position of resource specialist at a junior high school in West Los Angeles. To my surprise, I was placed as the number one candidate on the list by the interview committee. However, the principal, after the second interview, informed me that he was under pressure to hire an African American and told me that if could state that I was black, he would hire me immediately. I was very angry at the statement made by the principal and resolutely replied, "I am a Pacific Islander, and if you cannot hire me based on my merit then so be it." That evening, I shared the result of the interview with Shirley. Neither one of us could believe that here we were fighting for justice and equality, only to be told that we were not the right minority.

My disappointment and anger was short lived. The following week, I received a call from the principal of Palms Junior High School, who said he had seen the results of my written test for the position and wanted me to come in for an interview. Palms was also located on the west side, between Venice and Westwood.

When I arrived at approximately five o'clock, Dr. David Sowers, the principal, was the only one there to conduct the interview. He was a man in his forties with grayish hair and had an average build. Dr. Sowers greeted me with a smile and asked me to tell him something about my personal and professional self. The interview was long, with many detailed questions about special education and curriculum development. Dave Sowers' sense of humor made me feel at ease and broke the tension.

Toward the end of the interview, Dave asked questions about Fiji. He said that he owned a condominium in Kona, Hawaii, and spent every summer there. We continued discussing the island life and foods for at least an hour. When our conversation was over, Dave asked, "When do you want to start?" His question left me speechless for a moment. He said he would call my principal and let him know that he wanted to hire me and would appreciate a transfer within two weeks. I thanked Dave for his confidence and promised him that he would be very proud of his decision to hire this island boy.

Gary Peterson, the principal of Sun Valley, was aware of my search for a promotion. When he received the call from Dave Sowers, he was not surprised. The most difficult task now lay ahead of me: telling the students that I was leaving. I agonized over this for a while. On the Monday of my last week, I informed the students that I had received a promotion and that Friday would be my last day.

The news about my pending departure was greeted with anger and tears. One student became so enraged that he cursed at me and ran out of the class. He came back later in the afternoon and apologized. "I don't know what to do after you leave, Mr. Lal. You are our friend and teacher who stays with us, comes to our house, and takes us places. Nobody before you treated us like that; they only looked at us as a bunch of crazies." I really did not have an answer, but assured him that they would have someone just as caring to replace me.

The following day, several parents dropped by to ask if it was true that I was leaving. They expressed their disappointment and at the same time wished me well in my new endeavor. Thursday was back-to-school night, a time to meet the parents and discuss the instructional plan for the year. In spite of the fact that I was not going to be the teacher for that class, I fulfilled my duty and attended. That evening, the students and parents surprised me with a party and gifts. I felt like a traitor and even worse when some of the parents said goodbye with tears in their eyes.

Driving to Palms Junior High School was a challenge because there was no direct way to get there from Sunland. On the first day, I left home at six in the morning, arriving at Palms at 7:30 AM. In the main office, I was greeted by the secretary, who introduced me to a number of teachers signing in or checking their mailboxes. Then Mr. Vernon Bidewll, a rather slender man in his fifties, shook my hand and introduced himself as the other resource specialist. He gave me a brief tour of the place and guided me to my room, a tiny place with barely enough space for ten chairs and a desk. It appeared that a regular classroom had been divided into two small rooms for small group or individual instruction.

Vernon explained that in the resource program, we tested students referred by their teachers for low academic performance. Students who performed two or more grade levels below their peers in one or more subjects or exhibited disruptive behaviors were usually referred for testing. Once qualified, the students received individual or small group instruction, depending on the severity of the disability. A majority of the students needed help in English and math.

The student population of Palms was predominantly middle to lower-middle class white with some Latino and a few blacks. In view of the fact that Los Angeles Unified remained a segregated school district, in 1978 a federal judge ordered the board of education to devise a plan to desegregate the schools. The size of the district predicated that in order to comply with the judge's orders, students had to be bussed from great distances to specific areas. Some students were bussed from inner-city Los Angeles to the San Fernando Valley, about a thirty-mile bus ride, while others needed a short five-mile ride. Black and Latino students from mid-city Los Angeles, Venice Baldwin Hills, and Windsor Hills areas were bussed to Palms.

To meet the needs of the incoming students who had been relegated to mediocre education for generations, faculty and staff at all schools were required to attend workshops and classes in how to teach minority and multicultural students. Veteran educators who had only taught one race and ethnic group had to learn to understand and be sensitive to other cultures. The irony of the integration plan was that students were only transported in one direction, from the inner city and poor areas to the suburbs and not vice versa. No students who resided in the exclusive all-white communities were bussed to the inner-city schools.

The intent of putting students on the bus and transporting them across town away from their neighborhood schools was to give the minority students the quality of education provided to their white counterparts. Somehow, perhaps by design, nothing really changed.

Minority students were subjected to long bus rides to schools where they were placed in classrooms with teachers who, for the most part, did not care whether the students experienced academic or social success. Usually, teachers assigned these students seats in the back of the classroom, clustered in one area. Meanwhile, for safety and protection from the majority white students, the minority students tended to hang around together during breaks. In essence, the only aspect of the minority students' schooling that had changed was the physical location and nothing else.

The hypocrisy of the so-called school integration also hit close to home. We received a notice from Sunland Elementary that our boys were selected to participate in the school desegregation program and would be bussed to an elementary school in Pacoima, a predominantly black and Latino school. My nephews, Maynie, and some of the Latino kids who resided in Sunland received similar letters.

Shirley and I immediately went to the school to speak with the principal. She informed us that the school district had randomly selected the students, and there was nothing she could do to change the situation. We responded, "How could this be random selection if the few minority students who were naturally integrating the school were all relegated to be bussed?"

Like most minorities who do not fight the system because they believe they cannot win, Maynord, as well as some of the other parents, relented to the bussing program. Shirley and I on the other hand threatened the district with a lawsuit on behalf of our children. Miraculously, after our conversation with the principal and a few telephone calls to staff at the district's central office, we received a letter that our boys would not be bussed.

Dhyan Lal

When the idea of bussing minority kids to white schools hit the news, parents in these communities demonstrated in front of schools carrying placards decrying that these students would ruin their schools by bringing deviant behaviors into their communities. School board meetings were packed with speaker after speaker denouncing the board's action and the judge's orders. If one did not know that this was Los Angeles in 1978, one would think that we were in one of the southern states during the civil rights movement. That year, two individuals from the San Fernando Valley who had run on an anti-bussing platform were elected to the board of education.

As the judge's order could not be ignored, the district had to proceed with the desegregation plan, despite the outcry from the parents of suburban schools. A side effect known as "white flight" began to emerge. White parents in the suburban areas who were adamant about not having blacks and browns in their schools sold their homes and moved out of the boundaries of the Los Angeles Unified School District. White flight caused a decline in enrollment in the suburban schools in the early 1980s, causing the closure of some schools.

Dave Sowers was a leader who did not judge people based on their race or ethnicity, but their character. He convened several meetings with faculty and staff to prepare them for meeting the needs of the new students. He asked the faculty to be sensitive to the cultural differences and not to jump to stereotypical conclusions about one's race if he or she did not perform well in class. He asked them to deliver instruction using various modalities to meet the needs of all students. Some teachers expressed hostility about having to change their teaching methods just to cater to some inferior students. Others asked for extra help in dealing with the new students because they had heard that these students only wanted to cause problems and were not interested in learning.

Being a resource specialist was different from regular teaching because of the added responsibilities such as testing each student separately, developing the individualized education plan, and convening special meetings with parents and conferencing with individual teachers regarding students' progress. Much like the special education classes, each student presented a different academic and behavioral challenge.

I relished the opportunity of working with students experiencing adjustment problems that resulted in low academic performance. Ironically, many of the minority students were referred to us for their academic deficiencies and behavioral problems. Some of the Latino students who did not understand the language were labeled as being learning disabled. By virtue of my own experience, I could identify with the plight of these students and could develop special strategies to meet their needs.

In a short time, my reputation for achieving success with difficult students spread throughout the school. Teachers and counselors referred students to me for academic as well as counseling services.

Dave worked part-time as a coordinator for California Lutheran University and asked if I wanted to teach classes in counseling two nights a week. I jumped at the chance to be a university lecturer. He knew that I had a master's degree in counseling and believed that that combined with my experience would make me a valuable asset to prospective counselors. I was already teaching special education classes on weekends at California State University, Los Angeles, twice a month, but could not pass the opportunity to earn extra money and gain further experience.

Anne Coniglio, the seventh-grade counselor, asked if I could test a young man who was constantly being referred to her for behavioral problems. I conducted a background check for an academic and behavioral profile of this student before meeting with him. My investigation revealed that Osama Sidaros was a thirteen-year-old student from Egypt who had been in the country for only two years. Although he had managed to learn to speak English, his limited abilities in written communication and inability to assimilate into the school culture caused him to act out in classes.

Osama was a short, skinny young man with a dark complexion and a pleasant smile. When I met with him, he readily explained that he could not understand the teachers and that both the black and white kids made fun of his accent and picked on him. The test results revealed that he was slightly below grade level in mathematics but needed extensive help in improving his literary skills.

Osama's attitude, size, and overall demeanor reminded me of my own first encounter with the American society. I recognized that he had the zest for learning, but if his energies were not channeled in the right direction, he would gravitate toward negative tendencies. I advised him to receive permission from his teachers to come and see me anytime he wanted.

I had twenty-eight students on my official register, but in reality, I assisted twice that number on any given day. Students were bringing their friends to receive extra help. A large number of the bussed-in students sought me for extra help. During nutrition and lunch breaks, I mingled with and spoke to the students in the eating area. I became familiar with most of the students and knew a majority of them either by their first name or by a nickname. Knowing the students made it easier to break up fights or disperse the crowds in case of racial and gang problems. Students respond positively when called by their names.

One afternoon, Osama came running to me with a bloody lip and reported that he was accosted by a group of boys. He said he was sick of being picked on and was never going to come back. Reaching back to my own similar experiences, I asked him to calm down and think about handling the problem another way. I explained that it was time for him to fight back with more than his mouth.

I escorted him to the physical education teacher and asked the teacher to enroll Osama in a weight-training class. The teacher said that Osama could work to build his physical strength during class and after school. Osama enjoyed working out and in a short while began to show muscles in his skinny arms. With improved self-concept because of academic and social progress, by the time he was in the eighth grade, Osama became one of the strongest and most popular students in school.

I knew that, like Osama, there were many other students who needed that extra helping hand to get through the obstacles placed in front of them. Gordon McBain, the head counselor, enlisted my services to help the counselors with some of the problem students. I liked working with Gordon. Like Dave, Gordon was kid-oriented and wanted to give the youth every chance to succeed.

Gordon and I developed after-school and weekend instructional and social programs for the students. Dave was an avid runner. He ran at least eight miles every morning. He noticed that a number of students arrived at school around seven in the morning, and school did not start until 8:30 AM. Consequently, Dave initiated an early morning track club. Initially, many students joined the club, but the numbers declined rapidly. Few students could keep up with the daily eight-mile run. Osama was one of the few who ran with Dave at least three times a week.

# Chapter Twenty-Eight: The Path to Administration

In September of 1980, Dave and Gordon met with me and commented, "We are really impressed with the way you communicate with students and how you diffuse problems. We have an opening for a dean of students and wanted to know if you would like the position." Before I could respond, they said that I would have to help them in finding a replacement for my current position.

I responded, "Yes, I would love to be a dean, and I think I know a perfect person to replace me." As soon as I left Dave's office, I called Jeanette Gentis, my colleague from Carver. Jeanette had been at Carver for over twenty years and was ecstatic at the idea for a change in assignment and environment.

Within two weeks, Jeanette came to Palms as a resource specialist, and I moved into a large office as the dean in charge of student activities and discipline. At home, Shirley and the kids were ecstatic about my promotion. Technically, I was considered a teacher on special assignment because this was an in-house position and not one that was assigned by the district central office. Just the same, I functioned as a quasi-administrator with decision-making powers under the supervision of Gordon and Dave.

Some school policies were punitive and did not provide students with alternatives for success. With Dave's blessing, I was able to develop and implement positive discipline programs. For example, instead of being suspended for truancies and tardiness, students were mandated to attend after-school and weekend school beautification sessions.

My philosophy of having the students accept the responsibility for their actions and choose the consequence gave them ownership of the school. Students also felt that they were an important part of the institution. When students planted flowers, cleaned the buildings, and restrooms, they made sure that no one wrote graffiti or vandalized.

Some faculty members believed that students should be suspended for fighting, but I explained that giving them three days away from school did not solve any problems. Having the students talk out their differences and then putting them to work together built camaraderie and reduced tensions. I illustrated that "discipline with dignity" resulted in positive outcomes such as reduced truancies, graffiti, vandalism, violence, and overall disruptive behaviors.

Within a short six-month time period, the school culture changed from that of constant turmoil to a place where respect and order was the rule and not an exception. Slowly, the inner-city students began to feel welcomed and accepted in the school community. Every day I convened rap sessions with groups of fifteen students to discuss items ranging from their personal lives to what they liked and disliked about the school. They were asked to make suggestions on how to improve the academic and social climate. In addition, we organized after-school barbeques and sports activity sessions with parents. Dave's humanistic leadership style made our task of creating a friendly learning environment effortless.

The dean's position afforded me the opportunity to learn the practical aspects of school administration. I went to numerous meetings. Attending these meetings afforded me the opportunity to become acquainted with a number of administrators at all levels, including the superintendent. Gordon also took me to counselors meetings and asked me to assist him in developing the school's master program for course offerings. Both Dave and Gordon said that they wanted me to learn as much as possible in order to take the upcoming exams for the positions of head counselor and administrative dean.

Before the opening of the school in 1981, a parent came in with her son with transfer papers from another school. The paper stated that in view of his problems, Andrew Wolf was being given an opportunity to succeed at another school. Andy had been kicked out because he broke into the school and stole some electronic equipment.

After conferring with the dean from the other school and speaking with Andy and his mom, I decided to give him a chance to attend Palms. Andy was very quiet, gave one-word answers to questions, and kept his head down, rarely making eye contact. He was fifteen and tall and very muscular for his age. There was something about Andy that made me question the reason for his transfer from the home school. He did not appear to be the type of student who would engage in any kind of disruptive or illegal behaviors.

Andy's mother and father were teachers. He was brought up in a middle-class environment. After our initial meeting, I discovered that Andy's parents were getting a divorce. He felt abandoned, and breaking into the school was his way of acquiring attention. I introduced Andy to Osama; they instantly became friends and started working out together. In the meantime, Dave requested that I sponsor the school leadership group, the Palmarians.

The criteria for becoming a Palmarian were good academic and citizenship grades. One of the duties the members performed was to supervise the hallways during nutrition and lunch. There were times when gang members would sneak into buildings, threaten the monitors, and roam the halls writing graffiti or causing general disruption.

I approached Dave and gained permission to relax the rules and admit some students whom I thought had leadership qualities but did not meet the standards for being Palmarians. I promised him that they would be on their best behaviors, and I would accept the responsibility for their actions. My goal was to reward some students for changing their attitudes from negative to positive and to enlist the support of natural leaders. I was aware of a few boys who were forced into becoming gang leaders because they did not feel like valued members of the school. My new recruits, along with Andy and Osama, proudly wore their Palmarian sweaters and sashes and made sure that the buildings were secure. They also planned and successfully executed school activities.

With the success I was experiencing in my professional and family life, I felt like the luckiest person on earth. Len was also very proud of my continuing accomplishments. Every Friday on my way back from work, I would pick him up and bring him to our house to spend the weekend. He looked forward to vacationing at the house. To put it in his words, "I like being treated like royalty. My dinner is served; I swim whenever I want, sit outside and read, enjoy the company of my grandkids, and never have to worry about cooking or cleaning." The boys and Roshni, who was now three, looked forward to Len's visits. When he was around, they could get away with doing things that otherwise would lead to punishment. Len was a typical grandfather who liked spoiling the kids without having to discipline them.

One late Friday afternoon, after finishing my paperwork, I exited my office and headed toward the main office. The halls were dark with only the lights in the main office still on. No one except for the custodians was around. I went into the main office to sign out when I heard Dave's voice saying, "Dhyan, you're still here; come on in." He was reading a leadership journal. "You know, the exams for administrative positions will be given soon."

"Yes, I am trying to learn as much as I can about the various openings," I replied.

"Have you ever thought about getting a doctorate degree?" Dave asked.

I paused for a while and responded, "Not really." He proceeded to tell me about Nova University, which had won the American Association of School Administrators (AASA) award for the best doctoral program for practicing administrators.

With Dave's encouragement and support from Shirley, I enrolled in the doctorate program in September of 1981. We all knew that this new undertaking was going to be difficult and time consuming. The demands of the program were more than what I had expected. I looked to Shirley for assistance in conducting research and studying for exams. Studying for the doctorate became a family project. We found ourselves spending weekends at the UCLA library. The kids grew up to be Bruin fans.

Andy and Osama had become the leaders of the school. They channeled their energy into improving their academic performance. I treated them as if they were my own sons. They spent numerous weekends at my home and joined the family on vacations.

Sometimes, we had as many as six students spending the weekend at our house. Taking the young people away from their hostile and lonely environments and exposing them to the country-like setting of Sunland widened their horizons. I could see the changes in the behavior of the students during their visit and at school, especially in Andy and Osama.

I had been at Palms for a little over four years when I received a phone call in December of 1982 informing me that I had been assigned as the administrative dean at South Gate Junior High School. The students with whom I had started in the seventh grade had graduated and moved on to different high schools. Osama attended Hamilton High School, where he played football and joined the track team. Andy went to Venice High School and became interested in auto mechanics. He eventually received his bachelor's degree in mechanical engineering. Currently, Andy works for the State of California as the inspector for Bureau of Automotive Affairs. Osama received his degree in micro-conductor technology and has been working with numerous international companies.

My departure from Palms occurred during the winter break. On the first Monday of January 1983, I reported to my new assignment at South Gate Junior High School. The school lies in the southeast section of Los Angeles and is surrounded by industries. The ethnic population of the city of South Gate as well as the school is predominantly Latino.

South Gate was the largest junior high school in the country with a student population of approximately 4,200. Because of the size of the student body, the school was placed on a year-round schedule. Students were divided into three tracks and attended school for sixteen weeks with an eight-week vacation. At any given time, one-third of the students were on vacation.

The year-round schedule was fast paced and demanding. We were opening and closing a track every eight weeks. There were no long breaks or vacation times for staff. Essentially, we were running a factory with three shifts. The principal, Pete Ferry, a big man who stood six feet four and weighed over 250 pounds, made our work pleasant with his humor and caring, compassionate ways. Pete was at work by 6 AM and usually departed after 7 PM. He was a visionary who understood what needed to be done to provide quality education in such adverse conditions. Pete took a liking to me and respected my opinions on issues. We worked on projects to beautify the school, bring in monies to provide rewards for excellence, and recognize the faculty members who worked beyond expectations.

During the 1984 Olympics that were held in Los Angeles, I wrote to the chairperson, Peter Uberoth, and asked for his assistance in rewarding the students for their exemplary behaviors. From 1983 to 1984, the school had experienced an increase in student attendance and a decrease in truancies and gang violence. Mr. Uberoth sent us 2,600 tickets for students and chaperons to attend a number of Olympic events. The students were afforded the opportunity to partake in an experience of a lifetime. My sons and some of their friends attended several events, including the long jumps made by Carl Lewis.

In 1985, my dissertation on "reducing gang violence on school campuses" was accepted, and I received my doctorate degree. Of course, I could not have achieved this goal without the help of my wife and the understanding of my children. Pete Ferry was extremely helpful in providing me opportunities to conduct research on and off campus.

We had resided in Sunland for nine years and were yearning to move close to the beach area. After an extensive search, we decided to purchase a house on the Palos Verdes peninsula, an area south of Los Angeles. Moving from Sunland was difficult for the boys and especially traumatic for Roshni because she did not want to leave her friends and the house with a swimming pool. It didn't take them long to become used to the new area and make new friends. The boys enrolled at Rolling Hills High School, and Roshni entered the second grade in the neighboring elementary school.

My drive to work was somewhat reduced; however, Shirley's drive to East Los Angeles was longer. At times, she found herself on the road for approximately two hours each way. In August of 1986, my travel time was further reduced. I was promoted to the position of assistant principal at Dana Junior High School in San Pedro, only fifteen minutes from Palos Verdes.

The following school year, Shirley also transferred to a junior high school closer to home. Rather than spending all our time driving, we now spent more time with the kids. The boys were playing football and running track. In 1988, they broke many long-standing school track records and garnered quite a few first-place medals. Their best race was the 4 x 400 relay in which they won just about every competition and qualified for the state championship.

Dana Junior High is located a short mile from the Los Angeles Harbor in the once fishing town of San Pedro where the turf meets the mighty Pacific Ocean that pounds its waves against the rocks. The campus is built on a hillside with a main building on the street level and bungalows located on the terraced hill. From the third level of the campus, you can see the entire harbor with ships of all sizes either docked or moving in or out. Sometimes, two or three cruise ships can be seen coming in to dock early in the morning. I delighted in climbing the stairs to the third level to visit the classrooms and for the breathtaking view.

Students attending Dana came from diverse ethnic backgrounds. We had Greeks, Italians, Latinos, Yugoslavians, other whites, and few African Americans. Most of the students were from middle-class homes. Their parents were either working as longshoremen or were in some way associated with the shipping industry. The canneries of the old days were closing and being replaced by office buildings or expensive homes. Since the climate in the South Bay is mild year round, it is a very desirable place to live. In addition, the United States Navy and Air Force have large bases located around San Pedro, adding to the economy of the area.

Unlike the other schools, Dana presented some unique problems that required different approaches. A majority of the students were cordial, interested in school, and interacted with each other in positive ways. However, some students were belligerent and projected the attitude that they could do anything they wanted without having to face any consequences.

The gangs were formed along racial lines with a few exceptions where the membership was racially mixed. In a short time, I came to know most of the students, and they in turn went out of their way to introduce themselves to me. I immediately let the antisocial and delinquent students know that they could not hang around when the bell rang to go to class or smoke on school grounds regardless of the time of day.

In spite of the fact that a few students complained about the new rules and regulations, a preponderance of them adapted to the idea that if they committed an infraction, the consequences ranged from detentions to suspensions. I favored detentions because the time was used for cleaning and beautifying the campus, especially on Saturdays.

Regardless of the situation, there are always a few students who like to challenge authority figures. A tall, blond ninth-grade student decided he was going to smoke in the eating area during the lunch break. I approached the young man and asked him to put out the cigarette, explaining, "You know it's against the rules to smoke on school grounds."

I also noticed a pack of cigarettes in his shirt pocket and asked him to hand them over to me. He kept the lit cigarette between his index and middle finger and replied, "No, you can't make me stop, and I'm not giving you my pack of Marlboros." I reached toward his shirt pocket to retrieve the pack. He slapped my hand away and shouted, "Don't touch me, nigger!"

Instinctively, I placed both of my hands on the young man's chest and pinned him against the wall. "Don't you ever call me a name, you punk. And if you ever hit me again, I will break your arm."

A crowd had gathered around us waiting to see what would happen next. School police officer John Best saw the crowd and dashed toward us. When he saw that I was struggling with a student, he ordered the student to stop resisting. The student became more belligerent. Officer Best took out his handcuffs and cuffed the student's hands behind his back. "Now, if you behave, I will take off those cuffs, but if you keep on cussing and acting crazy, I will take you to jail," he said. Officer Best took the student to his office to obtain necessary information and record the incident.

Students were milling around engaging in animated discussions about the incident. A few of them asked me if I was okay. One said, "I saw what happened. He shouldn't have slapped your hand."

The sound of the bell signaled the end of the lunch break. I made my usual rounds encouraging students to be in class on time. As I was approaching my office, the school secretary informed me that the principal wanted to see me. As soon as I entered the office, the principal asked me to close the door and sit down. "You have only been here a week, and I have a complaint about you. A parent called and said that her son went home saying that the new black principal had just beat him up. She is going to call the board of education. Tell me what happened," she said.

I described the incident in detail and added, "In all my years in education, nobody has ever raised a hand to me. Plus, the other students were watching, and if I had backed down and did nothing, I would have lost all respect."

She seemed a bit uneasy about the whole situation. Finally, she advised me to be more careful about touching students and said, "I'll call the parent and let her know that I will handle the situation."

John Best came to my office smiling and said, "Man, you scared the shit out of that boy. I have been here two years, and this is the first time I have seen an administrator not afraid to take on these kids. They have been doing their own thing and getting away with a lot of mess, and it's about time someone put a stop to all of their nonsense. The word is out all over the campus that you don't want to mess with the new assistant principal; even the teachers are talking about it."

"Who was that boy, and why did he think he could get away with that kind of behavior?" I asked.

John replied, "This boy is sixteen years old. He was kept back, and I suspect he has been dealing drugs on campus."

That student never came back to Dana, but the story about the incident spread all the way to the district office. Jerry Malumaleumu, an advisor from the district office, made a trip to the school to meet me. "I had to come and see this crazy Fijian everyone was talking about," he said with a smile. "The word is out about your island style of dealing with the kids and that you make students come in on Saturdays to clean the campus, and the tardy problems have all but disappeared. Actually, a Samoan parent called and told me how happy she was with what is going on here now. She thinks you are Samoan."

Jerry and I spoke for a while sharing stories and of course talking about the Islands. He invited me to come to a meeting with some educators and concerned parents at a church in Carson.

Walking into the church brought back memories of the churches I used to attend back home. The building was an A-frame structure with round beam ceilings and walls that appeared to be made of the material used to make mats. For a minute, I thought I was in a church back in Fiji.

About ten people were seated at the table in the hall when I entered. They smiled and greeted me with "talofa," the Samoan word for hello. "We have heard a lot about you, and it is nice to finally meet you," said Saili, a teacher at Carson High School. Kathy, who was white and introduced herself as the honorary islander, taught at the local elementary school.

Reverend Taase started the meeting with a prayer and asked everyone to introduce themselves. The primary purpose of the meeting was to discuss the problems that the Samoan students were experiencing in the schools and to arrive at some solutions. Jerry and Saili were specifically concerned about the number of students getting into trouble at Carnegie Junior High and Carson High School.

"The students are roaming all over the place, and they don't even go to class. They get into fights with other kids and usually end up being suspended. The administrators don't know how to handle these kids, and the parents don't even bother coming to school to check up on them," Saili stated in an exasperated manner.

"We have the same problem at Carnegie. Parents are calling the district office asking for help," Jerry chimed in.

I listened to the concerns of the people and their frustrations of not knowing what to do. Reverend Taase finally turned to me and asked for some ideas. "You should request a meeting with the administration of both schools to express your concerns and offer some assistance in dealing with the youth," I suggested.

Reverend Taase thought it was a good idea and said that he would ask a couple of the ministers and chiefs to accompany him. He turned to Jerry and asked him to schedule meetings with the principals of both schools.

The city of Carson has the largest population of Samoans outside of Pago Pago, American Samoa. Although the children are born on the U.S. mainland, they are raised as if they were growing up in the Islands, with strict adherence to the Samoan culture and customs. Caught between two worlds, the children have difficulty switching between the American and Samoan cultures. To release their frustrations, the youngsters engage in disruptive behaviors at school, including joining gangs.

School officials as well as the parents were at a loss for what to do about the high rate of suspensions and low rate of graduation of Samoan students from the junior high and high schools.

At the next meeting with the Samoan community, I suggested that we have a luau to raise money for scholarships for the college-bound students. I enlightened the parents about the love mainlanders had for authentic luaus and suggested that we could charge at least $25 a person as a donation. "All I ask is that you cook the pigs in the ground and have traditional Polynesian dancing. The teachers and I will sell the tickets."

Reverend Taase replied, "People will not pay $25 to come to the luau. This community knows about the feast, and they will not pay more than $10." Some of the chiefs agreed with this.

"I understand that, but we are going to concentrate on the education community and the general population."

In the typical island style, the discussion lasted for about three hours. Every member presented an argument as to why the luau was either a good or not-so-good idea. I respectfully listened to the members. Finally, the decision was made to plan a luau for sometime in May to be held at Carson High School.

Since I was not familiar with the administrators of the high school, I recommended that the community leaders meet with the school staff and obtain permission to use the school auditorium. The leaders took my advice, met with the school principal, and were promptly turned down. Not knowing the political realities of a bureaucracy, the community again turned to me for guidance. At first, I was at a loss for ideas and figured that we were better off finding a small private location or to simply forget about the luau.

The harbor area was represented by a new school board member, Warren Furutani. I had met Warren at a meeting in San Pedro. He impressed me with his willingness to help the minority students gain equal footing in the educational arena. I decided to call Warren and express the concerns of the Samoan community. Unbeknown to me, Warren's father, Chuck Furutani, had worked with the Samoan youth in Carson in a program known as Teen Post. The Furutani name was well known in the Samoan community.

As soon as Warren heard the story about the luau, he volunteered to be the keynote speaker and said that someone would get back to me regarding the use of the high school. With Warren's name on the flier, we had little difficulty selling tickets. Three hundred tickets were sold in a short time. Miraculously, I received a telephone call from the principal of Carson High that it would be okay to use the school to hold the luau.

Thanks to Warren and the hard work of the community, the first luau held in 1997 was a success. At least 300 people were in attendance, and $4,000 was raised toward the scholarship fund. Eight students received $500 each toward their college expenses. It may not have been much money, but it was enough to provide the students with incentives. The community group adopted the name Association of Pacific Island Educators (APIE). The organization has held a luau every year, raising as much as $14,000 in 2002.

In August of 1988, I received a call from the local superintendent in charge of the schools in the South Bay. I was told that I had been promoted to the position of principal at Carnegie Junior High School in Carson. The news surprised and thrilled me at the same time. I called Jerry and gave him the good news. Jerry responded, "The community has been trying to get you over here ever since they met you. They were impressed with the luau and the way you deal with kids. Reverend Taase, along with several ministers and chiefs, went to see Mr. Furutani about you being assigned to either Carnegie or Carson. The principal of Carnegie left, so you were the right man for the job, Doc."

"How come you didn't tell me what was going on?" I asked.

"Well, we didn't want to get your hopes up in case things didn't work out," he replied with a chuckle.

Around 9:00 AM the next morning, I visited the school wearing a tropical shirt printed with hibiscus flowers, sulu, and sandals. The outside of the school was dirty with graffiti covering the walls and trees surrounding the school. When I entered the main office, a young woman with a pretty smile asked, "May I help you?"

"Yes," I replied in broken English. "I here to see principal about problem; he here?"

"No," she responded. "He is the new principal and will be here either today or tomorrow."

"Then who you?"

"I am Mrs. Garcia, the secretary. If you leave me your phone number, I will call you as soon as he comes in."

I muttered quietly, appearing to be angry, "Call him on phone. I need to see him. He should be here now."

Mrs. Garcia did not say anything for a while. Suddenly, she said, "Are you him?"

"Him who?" I inquired.

With a big smile and laughter, she pointed at me and uttered, "You are Dr. Lal. They told me you would do something like this." I could not maintain a straight face and admitted that I was testing the main office personnel and that I was impressed with her demeanor. Shaking her head and laughing, she said, "Welcome to our school."

Carnegie Junior High School was in disarray. The school grounds looked dreary; there were no flowers in front, and the grass had turned brown. I spoke with Becky about the possibility of planting some flowers and removing the graffiti. She was ecstatic about the idea and stated, "I have a friend who can give us flowers, and my husband is a plant manager; he would be happy to help."

On Saturday, Becky, her husband, my two sons, and I tilled the soil and planted flowers. Students passing by the school wanted to know what we were doing. "We are trying to make your school look nice," Becky replied. "That's Dr. Lal, your new principal. He doesn't want you to come to a school that is dirty and ugly."

"Can we help?" asked some of the strollers.

"Sure; we need all the help we can get," answered Merced, Becky's husband.

Before the day was over, we had approximately twenty students and adults helping with the planting of flowers and cleaning of graffiti. Each day, more individuals joined the beautification group, and about two days before the opening of the school, we were able to complete the beautification project. The graffiti had been removed, walls were painted, and the overall appearance welcomed the visitors to the campus.

It didn't take me long to witness the antagonism and hostility among the students. Different races of students hung out in designated areas with few groups mixing. The gangs, which were formed along racial lines, did not waste any time in sizing up each other and giving "hard" looks. A few fights took place during the first week, which prompted me to convene an assembly to speak with the students. My message to the students was, "The entire student body is a family, and we all are residing in a village on an island. We have to look after each other and make our village a happy, pleasant place. If you have a problem, come and see me. This is your school. Do everything you can to make this a place you can be proud of. Stop all the fighting and destroying the property; you are messing up your own pad. You must work together to show the rest of the world that you are not all fools and gangbangers." I met with the faculty and gave them a similar speech that spoke of a family working together for the betterment of the house.

In the evenings and on weekends, I met with parents and community groups to enlist their support in turning the school climate from negative to positive. On Sundays, I visited the various Samoan churches and spoke to the parents about taking an active role in the education of their children. A coalition was formed by the parents and students to safeguard the school and implement programs to increase student achievement. The leader of the parent group was a young Samoan named Faititi Simi, known throughout Carson as Kiki. Through his leadership and efforts, we were able to start evening and weekend academic and sports programs.

Thanks to Kiki, his brothers, Jerry Kaono of the Carson Sheriff's Department, and the rest of the community, Carnegie was transformed from an undesirable to a highly touted junior high school. During the next three years, students won a variety of academic and athletic awards, including a commendation from President George Bush for exemplary behavior.

All my life, I have heard people say, "No good deed goes unpunished," but I never knew what it really meant. I had spent three hard yet wonderful years at Carnegie and was ready to enjoy the fruits of my labor the following year. However, in August of 1991, I received a phone call asking me if I would accept a transfer to Carson High School.

At first, I was hesitant, but I accepted the transfer. As soon as I hung up, I called Warren Furutani to tell him about the transfer. "I'm the one who spoke to Bill Anton about getting you at Carson High," replied Warren. "Reverend Taase and several of the community members have been calling me to put you at Carson. You know they have a lot of problems, and you are the right man to take care of business."

"Thanks, Warren," I responded. "I'll do the best I can."

Except for the brief time I spent at Marshall High, frankly I did not have much experience working in a high school. After talking with Warren, I realized the faith the community had in me and that I had to do my best to improve the conditions at Carson.

Similar to Carnegie, Carson was a campus suffering from physical neglect and academic stagnation. The student population was diverse: 30 percent Latino, 25 percent Filipino, 25 percent African American, 10 percent Pacific Islanders, and 10 percent white. Inherent in the diversity was the jockeying for the control of the school by the various ethnic groups. The competition and rivalry to be the "top dog" increased tensions and usually resulted in fights. My first duty was to bring harmony among students and teach them to coexist peacefully.

At Carson High I had an advantage because I knew at least 35 percent of the students. They had previously attended Carnegie. I could not use the same introduction technique at Carson that I did at Carnegie. Gloria Markatos, the school secretary, had already called Becky and inquired about me.

The junior varsity and varsity teams were busy practicing for the opening game, which was three weeks away. It was a warm day, and there was a slight breeze coming from the west, but I could see the boys sweating profusely. They were engaged in a game-simulation practice in full uniform.

When I approached the field, I heard my name being called. Then there were a number of shouts of "Hey, Doc, what are you doing here?"

Someone yelled, "He's our principal." Players ran to the sidelines to welcome me with hugs and handshakes, bringing the practice to a momentary standstill. The coach decided it was time to take a fifteen-minute break.

Seeing the students and their enthusiasm made the problems that I was agonizing over inconsequential. I felt right at home. The students who had graduated from Carnegie during my first year were now the ball players and leaders of the school. Watching their reception of me made the other students who did not know me feel comfortable toward me. It was like a big family reunion. Some of the leaders from Carnegie—Sipou, Lomi, Chris Don, the Salima brothers, Charlie, and others—were on the team. Seeing them made me feel at ease and relieved. My worries about how to bring peace and harmony to the campus had just been simplified.

Gloria and I were discussing some items pertaining to the hiring of teachers when we heard noises coming from the far side of the building. Gloria stepped out to see what was going on. She came back and reported,

"There is a large group of football players heading this way. I think that is your welcoming committee.

"Students have been dropping by all summer inquiring about who the new principal was. A few kids said that they had heard in the community that you were coming here; they were very excited."

About twenty students came running in, and Sipou lifted me off the ground with a bear hug. He turned to Gloria and proudly stated, "This is our pops, you know. He was really cool and helped us at Carnegie. Now Carson's going to be cool and fun." All the others jointed in with Sipou's exhibition.

Gloria laughed and jokingly admonished Sipou to "put him down; you are squeezing him to death. Can't you see he cannot breathe?" At that moment, nothing could take away the joy and pride I felt. The boys bid farewell and headed home. Once the noise had subsided, Gloria said, "Becky told me that the only thing I had to worry about was kids coming to your office all day long, even when you're not here; now I know what she meant. I admire the relationship you have with these kids; they need someone like you."

"I love these kids; they really know how to make you feel good and show you their appreciation," I replied. "I'm happy to be here and look forward to a great first year."

There were many dynamic and dedicated people working at Carson. Once I was able to identify the heroes and the movers and shakers among the adults, my task became a lot easier. The school police officer, Willie Guillory, was one of those committed individuals who had graduated from the school, went on to college on a football scholarship, and after receiving his degree in criminal justice, came back to help the students. Willie was an African American who spoke Samoan. He was an essential figure on campus and in the community when it came to quelling racial or gang violence. He also was a volunteer coach for the football team.

With the help of the union leader, Richard Mangone, I was able to implement my interest-based-education and positive-discipline programs. With students taking ownership of their learning and behaviors, our task of improving the school became somewhat easier. Those teachers who didn't feel that students should have a voice in decision making were given the option of proposing a better plan or transferring to another school.

Some teachers openly voiced their dislike for my style of leadership, which included empowering the students, and left the school. Others who did not believe that the proactive and positive approach would last long hung around to see the results.

Within two short years, Carson High students were exceeding all expectations in their academic and athletic performances. The school received commendations from the Carson City Council and the State of California. Discipline problems, including gang and racial fights, were reduced by 90 percent. Student leaders under the guidance of the dean of students Fred Gardner and leadership teacher Robert Wareham established an on-campus court. Those students who wanted to challenge a decision could present their case in front of the court and had to abide by the decision of the court.

During the 1993 Los Angeles riots, all schools were asked to curtail any activities calling attention to race. Carson High students had planned a "Celebration of Diversity" week. When I announced that the celebration would have to be called off, the student leaders, including the gang leaders, argued that it was not a wise decision. They said that they had worked on the celebration for six months and canceling it would have a negative effect on the entire school.

After consulting my staff, we decided to go ahead with the planned activity. On that Friday, we had approximately 5,000 people enjoying the festivities. Warren Furutani opened the assembly by commending the students on their accomplishments and the pride they showed in their school and community.

Dances were performed by the African American, Latino, Pacific Islander, Filipino, and Southeast Asian groups. Various groups set up food booths and sold ethnic foods. Parents took an active role in the celebration by helping the students with the dances, food, and costumes. The event was highlighted in a half-hour PBS show titled *No Man Is an Island.* Because of the diligence of the entire student body and the community, there were no incidences of violence.

Success of Carson High School reached the White House. In 1993, President Bill Clinton presented me with a medal and appointed me to the White House Commission on President Scholars. Meeting and conversing with the president was an event that will be part of my memory forever. I found President Clinton to be extremely brilliant and exuding charisma.

The accolades and recognition I was receiving was dampened by Len's passing in 1993. He had been living in Texas with his daughter, Shirley, at the time of his death. I visited Len at least three times a year and kept in constant phone contact. He was ninety-three years old. I had lost him, but I knew that he was proud of me and would always be there to guide me.

I also received an exemplary leadership award from Leadership Education for Asian Pacific and was listed in the *Who's Who Among Asian Americans.* I could not have obtained the accolades without the participation of the faculty, students, and the community.

In the meantime, my wife and I published a book, *Handbook on Gangs in Schools: Strategies to reduce gang-related activities.* The popularity of the book among educators and law enforcement agencies resulted in requests for us to speak throughout the country. During our speaking engagements, we discovered that many of the problems occurring in schools were directly related to the alienation of students by the adults and the lack of parent and community participation.

Another success story of Carson High School involved a young man with a pleasant smile and superior athletic abilities. I was impressed with his sportsmanship and decided to take a look at his academic performance. Much to my surprise, he was not achieving the success in the classroom that he was on the playing field. I knew that with his talents he could receive a scholarship to a university. However, his grades were mediocre at best, just enough to keep him eligible for sports.

I summoned our sports hero, J. R. Redmond, to my office for a conference. He was polite, humble, and very responsive to my every suggestion. J. R. promised me that he would do better in his classes. He was one of the most popular students in school, and that was actually a distraction. In addition, J. R. lived in a gang-infested area that compelled him to identify with the neighborhood gang.

During one of my routine visits to the classrooms, I noticed that J. R. was absent from his math class. The teacher informed me that the young man had been absent for three days. I was perplexed because I had seen him at football practice the previous day. A summons was sent out by Gloria for J. R. to come and see me; he was nowhere to be found. I immediately put the word out to all the students that I needed to see J. R. and told the coach not to let him practice.

The next day, J. R. sheepishly came to see me. I did not say a word as I got up from my chair and closed the office door. Then I stood next to him and asked, "Where have you been for the past four days?"

He said, "In school."

"Boy, don't you know better than to lie to me? Now, I'm gonna ask you one more time, and you better tell me the truth."

"All right, Doc, I'm not gonna lie to you. My math and science are really hard, and I don't know what's going on, so I ditch and hang with my homies."

"Okay, here is the deal. I will speak with your teachers and see if you can make up the work. Also, you have to attend tutoring classes after school."

J. R.'s teachers agreed to give him makeup work and to provide him with extra assistance after school. He was pleased with the arrangement and continued attending classes without any absences for a few weeks. Unfortunately, his math teacher came to me and said, "I know you want to help the students, but some of them don't want to help themselves. Your boy J. R. has missed two straight days of my class and some of the other classes too. If he does not show up tomorrow, I'll fail him." I assured the teacher that I would definitely take care of the problem.

Immediately after the teacher departed, I called J. R.'s home without any success. I walked around the campus asking other students if they had seen him. Most of the students appeared to know his whereabouts, but were afraid to tell me. Finally, one young man said, "Don't be mad at him, Doc. There's been some problem in the hood, and he has to back up his homies. Dion, Ramon, and all the other DGAF guys are not here either. If J. R. didn't back up his homeboys, he would be a buster."

I thanked the young man and said, "You are great. I owe you one, so if you need anything, come and see me."

DGAF, or "don't give a fuck," was the gang in J. R. Redmond's neighborhood. The next day, I summoned most of the DGAF members and stated, "Look, I know that all you homies look out for each other, but J. R. is different. He is a gifted athlete who has a great future. If he makes it into the pros, he can help you guys and be a role model for the rest of the kids. You cannot drag him into stupid gang fights. What if he got shot, or some fool hit him from the back? If you really care for him, leave him alone and let him concentrate on his studies and football."

Finally, Dion, who was one of the leaders, looked up and said, "We hear you, Doc; you're right. I'll make sure that J. R. doesn't get involved."

I shook Dion's hand and thanked him for his support. As they were leaving, I requested that they tell J. R. that I needed to see him right away.

Before football practice, J. R. appeared in my office. "You wanted to see me, Doc?" he asked.

At first, I didn't say anything. I stood staring at him and shaking my head. Then I sat down, looked up, pointed my finger, and said, "I have had it with you. If you want to throw your life away, you're welcome to it. I have nothing to do with you and don't even want to see your face on this campus." The number one football player in Los Angeles was stunned. He stood slouching with his hand resting on the chair. "I want to see your father tomorrow to discuss your future."

With tears in his eyes, he mumbled, "I don't want to leave this school."

"What's the difference? You don't even go to class. Playing football is not the only reason for coming to school," I replied. "There is more to school than football. You must maintain your grades, work toward graduation, and meet the college entrance requirements. The rate you are going, you'll be lucky if you get out of high school. As of now, you cannot play football. Forget about going to practice today. I'll see you and your dad in the morning."

I was rough on the young man because I did not want him to think that he could slide on account of his athletic abilities. This was an exceptionally talented young man. He played many positions: running back, returning punts, receiver, defensive back, and quarterback. Regardless of their exceptional talents, all students were expected to abide by the school's code of conduct. I was trying to stress the importance of self-discipline to all individuals on campus, including those with exceptional talents.

The next morning I arrived early. Gloria informed me that Mr. Redmond and J. R. were there to see me. I placed my papers on the desk and welcomed them into my office. Gloria brought Mr. Redmond and me a cup of coffee. Mr. Redmond began the conversation by stating, "Dr. Lal, I heard that you had a conversation with J. R. yesterday and that you were very rough with him. He said that you threatened to kick him out of school, and he couldn't play football."

"You are absolutely correct," I replied. "He has been ditching school and hanging out with his gangbanging buddies. I like this boy; he is bright, a gifted athlete, and a very polite young man. However, he will never realize his dreams of playing professional football if he doesn't stop running with the gangsters. At the rate he is going, he won't even be eligible to play football this year. So I told him he can go somewhere else and mess up."

J. R.'s father looked at him and asked, "Is that true, boy? Have you been missing your classes?" Being an honest young man, J. R. did not deny any of my statements and simply nodded his head. "Well, Dr. Lal, you have my permission to use a two-by-four on his head if you need it to get him to class. I will take him home with me today, and we will have a heart to heart." I thanked Mr. Redmond for his prompt attention to my request for a meeting.

From the initial meeting, Mr. Redmond and I had established a relationship. We both kept an eye on his son and helped him to achieve his goal. I am an avid football fan and believe that team sports and winning attitudes build character. Once in a while, all of us have a tendency to take the easy road and need someone to guide us back to the right direction.

During the football season, J. R. and three other football players entered my office and promised me that he and his teammates would win the city championship for me. Faavae Faavae, the running back who was also the student body president, pointed his finger at me at said, "Yeah, Pops, we're gonna make it happen just for you 'cause you care about us."

I smiled, gave them hugs, and responded, "I really appreciate your gesture, but do it for the school and community."

*Not only did we win the championship in 1993, we defeated a team that had not lost a game in the semifinals. J. R. played the last minutes of the game with a severely bruised knee and a twisted ankle. He did not want to come out of the game, and he made the catch that led to the winning touchdown.*

*With assistance from the college counselor and his dad, J. R. passed his college entrance requirement, graduated from Carson, and received a scholarship to Arizona State University. He was heavily recruited by many major universities. During the 1996 football season, J. R. led Arizona State to the national championship game. After college, he was drafted by the New England Patriots of the National Football League. He played running back and made crucial plays that resulted in his team winning the league championship and the Super Bowl.*

*Mr. J. R. Redmond has never forgotten his humble beginnings. Soon after he won the Super Bowl, I called him to ask if he would come and speak to the students at Jordan High School in Watts. J. R. came to school the next day and spent three days on campus speaking with students about the importance of staying in school, obtaining an education, and becoming a role model for others. I am proud of J. R.; he is a role model and continues to help those in need. In 2004, J. R. signed with the Oakland Raiders, my favorite team.*

*The successes of students at Carson continued as increasingly students recognized that the school was only as good or as bad as they made it. They owned the school, and whatever they did reflected on the school and the city, good or bad. I am happy to report that my three and a half years at Carson were the happiest years of my thirty years in education.*

# Chapter Twenty-Nine: Meteoric Rise and Fall

I had been traveling within the state and nationally touting the success of Carson High School and strategies to reduce gang violence on campuses. My accomplishments were brought to the attention of Delaine Eastin, the Superintendent of Public Instruction of California. In January of 1995, Superintendent Eastin called and asked if I would be willing to go to Sacramento for a chat about the possibility of me working at the state level. I jumped at the request and headed to Sacramento the following week.

As I walked into the superintendent's office dressed in my finest suit, I said to myself, "I sure wouldn't mind working here." Delaine greeted me and introduced me to Sonia Hernandez, a deputy superintendent. Sonia initiated the conversation by saying, "Delaine and I have been hearing a lot about your work and are impressed by your energy and enthusiasm. Also, I have read your book on gangs, which is very good." All I could think about was that I was sitting in the office of the superintendent of the entire state.

After a few more minutes of conversation, Delaine asked, "Dhyan, how would you like to work with me?"

I was dumbfounded. "You mean as an assistant or a consultant?"

"No," she replied, "as the deputy superintendent of the specialized programs branch." For a second, I had to pinch myself to see if I was awake. "I think with your experience and reputation, you will be ideal for the job," she continued.

Sonia chimed in, "And if you need any help, you can always ask me."

"Sure," I said, "I would love to work with you. This is an opportunity of a lifetime."

I virtually floated out of the office at the conclusion of the interview. The island boy was just asked to be one of the deputies for the Department of Education for the State of California. I telephoned Shirley and gave her the good news. She was ecstatic and said that she had a strong feeling that something incredible was going to happen.

When I arrived home, I called bhai to give him the good news. In his typical proud voice he responded, "I was telling your mother you're gonna go far." After I hung up the phone, I wished that Len were still alive to see that his son was going to be the highest-ranking Asian/Pacific Islander in education in California.

On the airplane, all I could think about was how I was going to tell the students and the community in Carson about my pending departure. For the past eight years, the community had embraced me and helped me in every endeavor. How could I leave those children who depended on me and looked to me for guidance? How about all the young teachers who had committed to work at the school and the parents who were looking forward to sending their children to Carson High?

It was very difficult to leave Carson. The day I told Becky Garcia that I would be parting at the end of the following week, she could not stop crying and walked out of my office. She was the first one I informed. I asked her to keep it quiet until I had a chance to tell the rest of the faculty and staff. Well, two minutes later, one of the other secretaries came in and asked why Becky was crying. Within one hour, the entire school and community knew about my intention to leave. Oh yeah, the island grapevine was alive and well in Carson.

The following morning, I made the announcement about my promotion to the entire school over the public address system. Many adults and students could not believe that I would ever leave the school. One teacher put it quite plainly, "This school is your home, and you are a father, brother, and mentor to us. Nobody thought that you would leave your village here in Carson; you are the chief." I was lost for words and could only shake my head in agreement. Some students cried, while others made me promise to come back for graduation.

My notice to school personnel and students was short, but somehow they managed to organize a huge farewell party. Becky, the administrators, and Shirley had contacted the city officials and acquired the Carson Community Center for an "island style" farewell party. Approximately 600 people, some from as far away as Hawaii and Florida, were present. The festivities included a variety of food, hula dancing, and my friends taking the time to toast me. With tears in my eyes, I bid farewell.

Sacramento is approximately 400 miles from Los Angeles. Commuting every day to the state capital was out of the question. I had to acquire an apartment for the weekdays. Luckily, my cousin Suresh had just purchased a house in Sacramento. I figured that I would stay with him for a week or so and then find an apartment. Suresh would not hear any nonsense about an apartment. He was adamant that I stay with him. "Look, we are brothers, and if you are working here, you stay with me, just like my father lived with bhai."

I was thinking, like an American, that I was an imposition on Suresh and his family. Suresh never even entertained the idea of me living in an apartment. "I would be ashamed if you did not stay here," he continued. "You are older and have the right to stay in this house." I relented to his request and spent the next fifteen months with a brother that I had barely known.

Shirley was working as an assistant principal of a high school about thirty miles from home. Her job kept her at work until late in the evening. Roshni was only sixteen, and we did not want her to come home to an empty house after school. Therefore, we decided that Shirley would quit her job and stay home. We believe that children need their parents at all times, not just when they are babies.

Mother and daughter enjoyed doing things together without Daddy interfering with their every move. Although she was not driving to work, Shirley continued to be a consultant and an advisor for graduate students seeking doctoral degrees. Her leisure time was cut short when she was asked to teach a class for California State University, Dominguez Hills. That one class eventually led to a full-time position.

Working at the California Department of Education was significantly different from anything I had ever done before. The specialized programs branch was the largest division in the Department of Education with 1,200 employees. My responsibilities included the supervision of ten different departments and the state special schools. At least two days a week, I was traveling to some corner of the state speaking to groups and organizations or meeting with district officials or politicians. I had a personal secretary, three clerks, and a personal assistant who accompanied me to all meetings and took notes.

My experiences with the diverse group of people and situations gave me the opportunity to learn and understand the political realities of education. Before going to the state capital, I thought that all decisions were made with children in mind. I quickly learned that decisions were also made based on the number of votes it would generate. Politicians first take into account if the bills they propose would be received favorably by their constituents.

One specific incident that made me comprehend the politics of education was the class size reduction bill passed in 1995. I had argued that a bill passed five months before the beginning of the school year would not give schools and districts adequate time to prepare. The governor, however, signed the bill into law because the public thought it was a great idea to have smaller classes in schools.

It was an election year, and voters rewarded the governor for lowering the class size in elementary schools. Of course, they didn't understand the nightmare it created for the schools. Children were supposed to have small classes. However, schools had as many as forty students in one class with two teachers; thus calling this arrangement a reduction in student-teacher ratio.

The state's Department of Education provided assistance to local districts and insured that all schools followed state and federal guidelines in the delivery instruction and utilization of funds. If some districts were not compliant with state regulations, they were asked to make immediate corrections or face sanctions.

Compton Unified School District in Southern California faced financial as well as instructional deficiencies. In 1993, the state declared the district bankrupt and appointed a state administrator to oversee the total operation of the district. Delaine appointed me to oversee the district in 1996. During a meeting she said, "Dhyan, I need you to go and do your magic in Compton." Since I lived in Southern California, this assignment brought me back home.

The composition of Compton's administrators and the school board was predominantly African American. Political strife and corruption was rampant in the district as well as the city. Although the Latino population was rapidly increasing, they were not hired into management positions in the district. In view of the African American and Latino struggle, Delaine figured that a Pacific Islander would be considered neutral.

I was welcomed by all groups in Compton. I met with community leaders and parent groups to develop a strategic plan for the district. The school buildings were dilapidated, children had outdated or no textbooks, and the morale of employees was low. My responsibility was to bring about financial and academic sufficiency, as well as the inclusion of all subgroups in the educational process.

Streamlining the budget required reassignment of personnel, including relieving some high-ranking administrators from their duties. In conjunction with officials from the California Department of Education, the contract of the superintendent was bought out, and various assistant superintendents were assigned to school-level positions. Our actions resulted in immediate savings of $2 million.

Unfortunately, a majority of the central office staff was either related to or very close friends with some prominent politicians. Delaine was besieged by telephone calls from politicians, including members of the Black Caucus, complaining about the actions being taken in the district. I was asked to curtail my actions and proceed with political caution.

It was the political wheeling and dealing that had put the district in its current predicament. I tried my best to work within the system but found that there were roadblocks, no matter which direction I chose. I could not show favoritism and sacrifice the educational opportunities of the children. If I played the game, the children would continue to suffer, but the political pressure would subside. I decided to listen to my conscience and work toward creating a positive educational environment for children and adults.

My actions increased the pressure on the state and Delaine. Some politicians demanded that an African-American state administrator be placed in my position. The pressure finally became unbearable for the state superintendent. After six months, by mutual agreement, I resigned from my position. This was a very difficult and heart-wrenching decision.

Some members of the community, specifically the Latinos, objected to my resignation.

The deputy superintendent of Los Angeles Unified School District, Francis Nakano, heard about my resignation and asked me to come back to LAUSD and work with him. I was pleased to hear from Francis and accepted his offer. Francis was one of the founders of the Alliance of Asian Pacific Administrators, an organization that mentored and sought promotions for Asians. I was the only Pacific Islander administrator in the group.

Francis assigned me to work in the division of adult and vocational education. My responsibilities were multifarious, including working with high schools, alternative schools, occupational centers, and various county, state, and federal agencies pertaining to career education. The connections with people that I had made while working for the state were an advantage when I needed access to officials in public and private institutions. It felt good to be back home in LAUSD working with my longtime friends.

My return to LAUSD was short-lived. In August of 1997, the superintendent of Lynwood Unified School District, Audrey Clarke, called and asked to have dinner with Shirley and me. Audrey was our professor at CSULA in the mid-seventies. She was a handsome and extremely bright black woman who had worked her way up from teacher to superintendent.

During dinner, she said, "I would like you to work with me as the deputy superintendent. I have followed your career and am very impressed with your accomplishments. Your experience in working with the people from the state and what you did in Compton are very valuable. I need you to come and help me with some instructional and personnel matters."

Shirley and I thanked Audrey for her offer and asked if we could talk about it at home. "I really appreciate your confidence in me and think it would be a pleasure working with you. However, I just came back to

LAUSD a year ago and don't think it's wise to leave again. But I'll get back to you in a couple of days."

"No rush," Audrey replied. "Take your time. I am sure that whatever you decide will be in your best interest."

On the way home after dinner, we deliberated on Audrey's request. I knew that if I remained with LAUSD, I would move through the ranks within a few years. However, the opportunity to work with Audrey as her second-in-command was also very appealing. Following a lengthy discussion where we weighed the pros and cons of leaving or staying, we decided that I should take a chance and join Audrey.

Walking into the central office of the Lynwood School District affirmed our decision to accept Superintendent Audrey Clarke's offer. The staff was friendly and appeared to be dedicated to providing the best possible educational opportunities for the children. This was a small school district with approximately 16,000 students.

Similar to Compton, Lynwood was experiencing a demographic shift in population from that of being predominantly African American to Latino. Nonetheless, a majority of the administrative staff was African American. Audrey was attempting to employ and promote Latinos, but encountered resistance from the governing board, which was comprised of three African American and two Latino members.

The state's Department of Education had conducted an audit of some of the educational programs and found the district in violation of numerous state and federal guidelines. I was given full control of running the district and would only answer to Audrey.

To correct some of the non-compliant problems, I asked Audrey to relieve the assistant superintendents of business and human resources from their duties. These individuals neglected their duties and were a detriment to district operations. We reassigned some members of the

 Dhyan Lal

staff and developed an organizational chart delineating clear roles and responsibilities.

Our actions were fruitful because in a subsequent audit, the state found that the district was taking corrective measures and moving in the right direction. Audrey and I collaborated on most of the decision-making process. We instituted professional development programs for teachers and administrators and provided incentives for teachers to seek further training.

With the consolidation of certain departments and the elimination of certain positions, we were able to put more money into the schools. Still, there was a shortage of teachers for bilingual education. Some of the members of the board decided they wanted to go to Spain to recruit teachers. I objected to this idea and suggested that we recruit locally to save money.

My objections about the trip to Spain combined with the alleviation of some central office positions did not make me very popular with a couple of the board members. I explained that we were maximizing efficiency and minimizing cost. Regardless of my explanations, they were angry about my actions—especially the member who was the nephew of one of the assistant superintendents whom I had recommended for termination.

Lynwood was also building a new high school, which when fully furnished and equipped with the latest technological equipment would cost $98 million. Audrey asked me to be responsible for the final stages of the project.

One night, a board member called me at home and suggested that a certain individual should be given the contract to lay carpeting in the school. I informed the member that we would follow the state guidelines for bids on contracts. She was very irate and muttered, "We'll see about that."

The following week, the three African-American members of the board called for an emergency meeting. During the closed session of the meeting, they discussed my role with the district and proposed that they would be better off without me. Audrey and the two Latino members objected. Nonetheless, with a 3–2 vote, the board decided to buy the remaining year of my contract.

My status was announced during an open meeting with approximately 600 parents and community members present. The audience vehemently objected to the decision, to no avail. I quietly left the room. That night, the audience became unruly and the police had to be called. During the next election, all three of the members were defeated.

Despite being disappointed, I took my predicament in stride and used the time as a freelance lecturer. I conducted seminars in strategies to turn around low-performing schools and districts and to reduce gang violence on campuses. I also spoke at conferences on the topic of effective leadership.

# Chapter Thirty: The Unexplainable Tragedy

It was December of 1997, and my father had been ill. He was diagnosed with having pneumonia. When Shirley and I visited him in the hospital, he was lying there with tubes inserted in his nostrils and a breathing mask attached to his face. As soon as he saw us, he attempted to pull out the tubes and the mask. We held his hand and told him to leave them alone and that he would be fine in a few days. He squeezed my hand as if to say, "I hate this; get me out of here."

Bhai was not the kind of person who sat idle; he was always doing something. I knew that he hated lying there like an invalid, helpless. I held his hand and said, "You'll be out of here in a couple of days. In six days, it will be Christmas. We'll celebrate it with a big party." He didn't really respond, but squeezed my hand.

Gautam and his wife came down from Portland to visit bhai. They were staying with Gyan in Marina Del Rey, which was close to the hospital. Bhai still had some congestion in his chest and the hospital wanted to keep him a little while longer. On Christmas Eve, I decided to go to the hospital for a visit. However, after being stuck in traffic for two hours, I called Gautam to say I was going to be late. He said, "We just came back

234

from the hospital. Bhai is doing fine. Go home, and we can go see him tomorrow."

On Christmas morning at about 4:50 AM, the phone rang. Shirley and I looked at each other; we knew it was bad news. Our feelings were correct. Gyan's oldest son, Niraj, was on the line crying. He said, "Bhai passed away this morning; the hospital just called us."

When we entered Gyan's house, we were greeted with loud cries and hugs. Amma was sitting in the corner of the living room with her hands covering her face; my sisters were crying and saying, "Why did you have to leave us?"

Gautam was sitting in a chair shaking his head with tears flowing down his cheeks. "Man, I wanted all of us to celebrate the holidays together. I thought that our parents were getting old and we should celebrate while they are still alive. Now bhai is gone, and I never got a chance to say the final goodbye."

Bhai was the glue that held us together. He was the patriarch of the entire Fiji clan. His passing symbolized the end of an era. Everyone came to him for advice. He was the voice of reason in disputes. The grandchildren who had never been to Fiji often gathered around him and asked about his life in the Islands when he was a boy and what it was like living in a hut without all the modern conveniences. He took a great delight in telling stories, especially the ones about his fishing expeditions.

Within an hour, approximately fifty people were at Gyan's house. Gautam, Shirley, and I decided to go make all the funeral arrangements. Since it was Christmas, locating individuals to make the arrangements was a bit challenging. Nonetheless, we managed to make the necessary transactions.

I was extremely morose but knew that I had to be strong for the rest of the family. To keep us from crying, Gautam kept making jokes when we bought items for the funeral. During the purchasing of the shirt, suit, and casket, Gautam turned to Shirley and me and said, "Remember, when I go, I want you guys to buy me the same thing. I want a suit just like that one."

I said, "Sure, you can have anything you want, but let's take care of bhai for now."

"Just don't forget," he responded.

Gautam knew that if he didn't keep things lighthearted, Shirley and I would probably break down like all the others. He was the eldest, and the responsibility of keeping the entire island clan from "losing it" was his responsibility. He even made the owner of the funeral home laugh with some of his quips.

A large crowd had gathered at Gyan's house by midday. The island grapevine had quickly spread the news. Most of the women were hugging each other and crying while the men sat with misty eyes. Stories about bhai's life were being told by various individuals. Everyone had something interesting to share. Yes, he was a unique individual, the last one in his family to find his resting place.

A throng of people kept coming and going from Gyan's house throughout the day. Shirley and Roshni left for home at about 10:00 PM. Amrit and I stayed behind to be with the family. Gautam was keeping people laughing with his jokes, saying that bhai would want us to have fond memories of him and celebrate life. It was approximately two in the morning, and nobody had slept a wink. Amrit and I decided to go home and sleep for a couple of hours.

We were getting ready to depart, and Gautam kept insisting that we stay because he wanted to spend time with everyone. I said, "We're going home to grab a few hours of sleep and will be back."

"Oh, man, why do you want to leave me?" he replied. We stuck around for about fifteen minutes and finally said good night.

No sooner had my head hit the pillow than the phone rang. I turned to Shirley and said, "Who the heck is calling this early in the morning?"

"Hello, hello," I yelled.

Finally, I could hear someone crying. It was Niraj. "Uncle Dhyan," he said, "Uncle Gautam passed away. He had a massive heart attack."

"What, what," I said. "We'll be right there." Shirley and I jumped out of bed completely astounded and quickly put on our clothes. "How could this happen? Yesterday he was laughing, telling everyone to remember the good times with bhai and that he would want us to celebrate life not mourn his death."

The sun was attempting to peek through the clouds as we pulled into the parking lot of the hospital. As we were walking in, Ashok and Gyan came out crying. Without saying a word, we hugged each other and expressed our sorrow and disbelief. Shirley and I went in to look at the body. At this point, I could not contain myself, and tears flowed freely down my cheeks. What I was seeing was not true; he was simply sleeping. After all, I had just left him no more than three hours ago.

I could barely walk to the car because of the shock. How could this happen? Gautam came to celebrate the holidays with the family; instead, we found ourselves in mourning. Bhai was suddenly taken from us. As if that wasn't enough, approximately twenty-four hours later, Gautam died in the living room of Gyan's house in front of everyone. Amma, who was already depressed, went into shock. She pounded her fist and begged someone to revive him.

I couldn't deal with the sadness, confusion, and especially amma's condition, and walked outside to gather strength. If I stayed inside, I would have broken down with the rest of the family. Someone had to be strong. The whole family was out of it. They did not know what to do. Munni, Gautam's wife, sat motionless in the corner with her eyes open staring into space.

Hundreds of people gathered at Gyan's house after hearing about Gautam's death. Shocked and perplexed, they stood around in silence not knowing what to say. The deafening sounds of cries from the women filled the air. There was hardly a dry eye anywhere.

My cousin Suresh, Shirley, and I gathered our senses and proceeded to go and arrange for another funeral. The owner of the funeral home could not believe why we were there. He said, "You mean the gentleman who came with you yesterday and was making the jokes?"

"Yes," I replied. "We cannot believe that this is really happening."

Gautam must have known something. Although I am not religious or believe in spirits, I think my brother knew something. Did he have a premonition? He didn't want my son and me to leave him on Christmas night, saying, "Why do you want to go so soon? Stay with me a little while longer." He talked about celebrating life and not wasting time "crying over spilled milk."

The word of Gautam's death spread to our relatives throughout the world. Friends and family came from Australia, Canada, New Zealand, Germany, England, Fiji, and many other parts of the world. After all, two legends from Fiji were no longer with us. Their deaths left an indescribable emptiness.

On the day of the funeral, over 700 people came to show their respects. The crowd spilled out of the funeral parlor and into the streets. The owner of the funeral home stated, "I have been doing this for twenty years, and I have never seen anything like this." His statement was echoed by some of my colleagues who had come to pay their respects.

An eerie feeling permeated throughout. Seeing father and son lying there in caskets next to each other made saying goodbye difficult. It appeared as if they were taking a nap and would rise any minute. I overheard some people saying that bhai and Gautam were very close and they decided to leave together. I was perplexed and could not think about anything. All I knew was that lying there were two loved ones who brought so much pleasure to people when they were alive and so much grief when they died.

According to their wishes, my father and brother were cremated and their ashes spread into the ocean. My son Amrit, Niraj, and I swam out to the deep portion and slowly spread the ashes. When we were finished and ready to swim back, two dolphins came within a foot of us, made what seemed to be laughing sounds, and played. They circled around us a few times, jumped, and swam away making the happy laughing sounds.

When we came back to Gyan's house, we told the story about the dolphins to some of the elders. They said that the two dolphins were bhai and Gautam letting us know that their souls were at peace and that they were happy. I am not a religious man, but I do believe the dolphins were the reincarnation of my father and brother. I have never forgotten that scene in the ocean that day.

I did not cry all during the entire tribulation, but broke down on my way home. The two people in the family who were most instrumental in my journey to America were gone. They were my pillars of strength. Bhai and Gautam were admired and respected by the Fijian/Indian community. Their legacy from Fiji carried on into the new land.

Chapter 31: Here We Go Again

Again, I spoke with my good friend Francis Nakano at LAUSD, who gave me an assignment as the administrator of the health and human services division. I gladly accepted the position because I welcomed the challenge and enjoyed working for Francis. In this position, I learned the specific roles nurses, psychiatrists, psychologists, social workers, and professionals play in education.

Right at about this time, the Los Angeles Unified School District had an election. Four out of seven new board members were elected. Election of the new majority was financed by billionaire Eli Broad and his friend, the millionaire mayor of Los Angeles Richard Riordan. The gentlemen sought the control of the school district and its $10 billion budgets.

The new board moved quickly to remove the superintendent and his cabinet and bring in their own people under the guise of reorganization. Meanwhile, the state legislature, which had been growing tired of mismanagement of funds by the district and low academic achievement by students, sought to break LAUSD into smaller districts. Parents and local communities complained that the central office was out of touch with reality and did not understand their needs.

An interim superintendent, Ray Cortines, was hired to devise a plan that would create local districts and keep the central bureaucracy intact. Cortines put forth a plan to reorganize the district into eleven local sub-districts with its own superintendents. His idea was, in reality, a rehashing of the old system where the district had seven areas with a superintendent leading each area. Under the proposed plan, the local district superintendents would answer to the general superintendent who was employed by the governing board.

If there is one thing I have learned in thirty years in education, it is that the more things change, the more they remain the same. As one of my colleagues put it, "Here they go again, rearranging the chairs on the deck of the *Titanic*." Every time there is a question about the enormous size of the district and the inability of the central office to provide adequate leadership, a restructuring plan is put into effect. I have seen regions, areas, clusters, and local districts. Do these restructuring efforts affect the schools in any way? No; if anything, the schools are burdened with more paperwork and supervisors who find ways to justify their jobs.

I was not pleased with the direction in which the central office was going. In a conversation with Francis, he confided in me that he was not going to be a part of a plan to destroy the culture of LAUSD and would be retiring. "You know, Dhyan," he said, "I have spent thirty-five years with this district and am proud of my accomplishments. I think it's time for me to retire and do the things that I have been putting off all these years.

"Here's my advice to you. Take a position as the principal of a high school. There are many schools that need your expertise. You will be doing what you like best, working with the high-school kids. If you really want a challenge, take over Jordan High School. The principal is retiring within a month. You will be the ideal choice for that school."

"You have done so much and helped so many people, it will be difficult to see you go," I replied.

In February of 2000, Francis retired, and I accepted the position of principal of Jordan High School in Watts. I was a bit apprehensive about assuming the leadership of one of the lowest performing and the most violent schools in the district and state. After all, I had been a bureaucrat for five years with very little contact with school sites.

Jordan High School is located in Watts, one of the poorest neighborhoods in Southern California. Factories and the Jordan Downs Housing Project surround the school. Jordan has historically been one of the lowest performing high schools in the district and state. The student population is 75 percent Latino and 25 percent African American.

When I arrived at Jordan High School, I found a school that was in total disarray. The buildings were covered with graffiti, little or no grass was visible in the quad, and the eating area was filthy. The benches and tables were so old and dirty that students stood up to eat their lunches. Student morale was extremely low, to say the least. The look of hopelessness and helplessness was evident on the faces of the students.

Gang fights were a daily occurrence. On my first day, there were four gang fights and a food fight during lunchtime. When I asked a few of the students why they exhibited such behaviors, they replied, "Nobody cares about us; we have to do whatever we can to survive." They pointed to the benches, dilapidated buildings, filthy restrooms, burned-out areas of the campus, and the dirt that was known as the quad.

"Why have a food fight?" I asked.

"Look at this dried meat and hard bun; you call this food?" one student responded, showing me his hamburger.

I promised the students that I would do everything in my power to create an environment where they would feel safe and feel that it was their school. They responded, "We have heard these promises before. Just because we live in the projects, all we get is lip service."

I assured them that this was not an empty promise. "Look, I do not want to work in such a depressing environment, and I don't expect you to attend a school that is in such deplorable conditions."

Repeated requests by me from the district offices to repair the items went unheeded. Someone from the community contacted Randy Paige, the investigative reporter for KCBS television channel 2, and informed him of my efforts. Randy approached me and asked, "Are you willing to talk about the problems facing Jordan on television and expose the district?"

At this point, I was exasperated and said, "I would not want my son or daughter attending a school that looks like this; why should I expect anything different for these children?"

Randy's report regarding the dilapidated conditions of Jordan High School was shown on the evening news in three-minute vignettes for a week. The morning after the first segment of the report was televised, a number of individuals from the Los Angeles Unified School District central offices came to the school to meet with me. They stated that Superintendent Roy Romer was very upset about the televised report and sent them to speak with me about the repairs.

The student body president also appeared at a LAUSD board meeting and announced, "It is demoralizing to go to school at Jordan because it is rundown and dirty."

Another student told board member Mike Lansing, who represented the Jordan area, "Jordan High is so bad that it should be blown up."

A massive renovation effort was immediately put into motion. New grass was planted, leaky roofs were repaired, and all classrooms and buildings were repaired and painted. The cafeteria was completely renovated and outfitted with new equipment. Students had a voice in selecting the cafeteria menu.

As the students saw the changes taking place, they acknowledged that I had kept my promise. While walking across the quad one day with the director of high schools, Andreda Pruitt, I heard a student yell, "Dr. Lal, thanks for making this into a white school."

Andreda shook her head and said, "That's a shame and tragic that these young people think a nice-looking school is only for white kids."

"But that's all they have known all their lives," I responded. "They have accepted the fact that they are not entitled to quality education in an environment that is conducive to learning."

Within a year, Jordan was transformed from a "ghetto school" to a school that could have been located in any suburban community. Students took the responsibility for ensuring that the buildings were free from graffiti and other forms of vandalism. Leaders of the local gangs met with me and pledged that they would tell their members to curtail the gang activities. One member simply stated, "Hey, man, we like what you're doing trying to help our brothers and sisters. We don't want to mess up anything."

Some of the veteran faculty and two of my staff members didn't like my idea of empowering the students. At a meeting, I let all the adults know that we were a team working for the common goal of making the school a better educational institution. I said, "This team is going to the Super Bowl, and we will do everything in our power to provide our students every opportunity for success. If you cannot meet this team's demands of hard work, which includes working on Saturdays, you can be a free agent."

Several of the faculty members decided that I was asking too much of them and decided to transfer to another school. Working with Janet Salem, the assistant principal, I was able to hire approximately thirty new teachers who were willing to spend time with the students and were not afraid to take on the challenges.

Not only were the students academically deficient, the performances of the athletic teams were abysmal. The girls' soccer team had not won a game in five years, and the boys' soccer team had won only a few games. I hired a new soccer coach, who led the girls' and boys' teams to championship games in successive years. Robert Dinh was a compassionate biology teacher and a coach who knew how to get the best performance out of his players. Robert was a Vietnamese man who came here as a boat person and went on to West Point.

It doesn't take a genius to realize that education is a function of economics. Children whose parents have the economic means are provided with all the opportunities for success from the time they are born. Because they have more resources, the children in the upper and middle classes receive better education. Although the government has tried to bring some degree of equality to inner-city schools through allocation of funds for specific programs, most of the monies appropriated go into people's pockets in the form of salaries and consulting fees instead of helping the youngsters.

So again, children going to school in the inner city are right back where they started, two strikes against them before they even step up to the plate. Most don't have enough to eat, some live in cramped quarters, and others live in group homes. They suffer from emotional and psychological problems.

These kids come to school with their baggage full and ready to bust, and we try to shove some more stuff into the baggage until they explode. Students give up mentally, eventually socially, and physically as well. Sometimes they display their anger and frustrations by fighting, disobeying authority figures, and dropping out of school.

Rather than letting us know that they have too many problems, they engage in disruptive activities. We deal with their symptoms by attempting to devise programs that we think may help them become better people. Their behaviors create problems in the school and the community, but nobody really looks at the real problem. I strongly believe that caring and hardworking individuals can instill a sense of pride and ownership among students, thus showing them the alternatives to drugs and violence.

Successes of Jordan students were directly related to the diligence of the faculty and staff. Jordan's Academic Decathlon Team gained 20,000 points from the previous year, finished twenty-second, and received the most-improved team award, a feat never before accomplished. For the first time in a long-standing history of failure, 70 percent of the graduating class of 2003 enrolled in a four-year university, and 20 percent enrolled in community colleges. The science department won six city and state academic competitions, including placing twelfth in the nation in the robotics competition. Moreover, the number of student suspensions and opportunity transfers decreased by 60 percent over the previous years. Most significantly, there were only ten fights on campus; this reflected a 95 percent reduction from previous years.

A former high-school principal was appointed as the superintendent of the schools in Watts. On her first visit to Jordan High, she dictated to me that she was the superintendent and I had to do what she said. She did not care about the fact that the school had shown academic and social improvements. Her directives to me were to be a follower and not attempt to lead because she was the leader.

She already knew about me, and it was evident that her mission was to demean and defame me. The students and faculty were never acknowledged by the superintendent for their accomplishments. However, in June of 2003, I received my reward: a transfer to a middle school. When I approached the superintendent and asked for the reason for my removal, she replied, "Failure to improve the school." All statistics showed just the opposite.

The indisputable reason for my transfer was because I was the only non-African American principal in the secondary schools and the only one to achieve success. Additionally, the television feature exposing the deplorable conditions under which students from Watts were expected to attend school added to her displeasure.

The superintendent and other LAUSD personnel did everything possible to make me leave Jordan High and the LAUSD. Since I did not leave Jordan despite the continuous harassment, the superintendent removed me as principal. A colleague of mine who was on her staff told me that she said, "Who does he think he is trying to act smarter than us? He is not one of us; I'll fix him."

All non-African Americans who had helped turn around the school were either removed or transferred to another school. Janet Salem, who is from the Middle East, was sent to another school. Julie Neilson, the college counselor who personally drove students to colleges as far away as Berkley, was removed. Julie is Jewish. Saul Sandoval, a Latino counselor and co-sponsor of the Heritage Club, was removed, and Marvin Avila, assistant principal, who is from Belize and worked tirelessly to increase attendance and decrease violence, was harassed to the point that he had to take a medical leave of absence.

We were transferred because the superintendent felt only African Americans should be in charge. The progress made by the students and the involvement of the community was disregarded. I don't see color; I see children who need help, and I want to give them the assistance they need. After all, if it wasn't for Len, who didn't see color, I would not be in the United States enjoying the opportunities this great country offers. Nevertheless, the narrow-minded individuals who practice reverse racism sacrificed the well-being of the children for their own pettiness.

People always ask me why I take such personal interest in the students, especially the needy ones, or "losers." My answer: "Someone once took an interest in me and brought me halfway across the world to receive quality education. I was a stranger, but he raised me like a son." I want to continue Len's legacy of helping those who are less fortunate. In helping others, we help ourselves.

# Epilogue

My adventure began forty-two years ago and is still continuing. The beginning of the journey was a bit rough, but each obstacle thrown in my path only helped me become resilient and stronger. Would I change anything if I could? I don't know.

The irony of facing reverse racism is another obstacle thrown on my trail as I continue my expedition. I cannot look back. The future presents challenges that require the fortitude I need to carry on bhai's and Len's legacies. They had seen something in me that compelled them to make the daring decision to have me continue my education in America. Could I send my thirteen-year-old son away with a stranger? I really don't think I could.

I am proud to have had the opportunities that this country has provided. Now it is my turn to help others pursue their dreams. In the Islands, our wealth is measured by how much one can give away and not by how much one can hoard. Len wanted me to choose a helping profession. I chose education because I knew that I could help those who, like me, needed the extra hand to guide them.

My wife and I have raised our children to appreciate what they have and to always help those in need. They were raised as Americans with middle-class values and received quality educations. Dhyan, the oldest, is the director of finance for a hospital in Los Gatos, California. Amrit is a high-school English teacher and football and track coach. Roshni, after receiving her master's degree from George Washington, is working at the Smithsonian Museum in Washington, D.C.

Shirley, after spending a few years in public school administration, pursued her goal of teaching at a university. Currently she is the director of evaluation for the School of Education at California State University, Dominguez Hills.

There are countless numbers of people who have migrated from Fiji and reside throughout the United States and Canada. Almost all of our relatives live in either one of these countries. Since I had departed Fiji at a young age, I still don't know all of the extended family. However, we always seem to get together during weddings and funerals.

After all these years, I cannot get my homeland out of my system. For the past six years, I take my vacations in Fiji. Usually I go alone, to capture what I missed during my childhood. Recently, however, Martin Sanchez, a professor friend from Berkeley; Phil Kuo, a friend of the boys; and Dhyan have joined me.

We stay with friends and relatives on the main island of Viti Levu and spend at least one week in a village on a remote island. This island has no electricity, water, or any of the other modern conveniences. We sleep in a hut, fish, and enjoy the real island life. I guess one can say that "you can take the boy out of the island, but you can't take the island out of the boy."

# About The Author

The author is currently a superintendent of a school district in Southern California. He has worked with handicapped students, youth at risk, and gangs. His work with youth gangs has brought him international accolades. His personal experiences with adversities while going to school in the United States steered him toward the teaching profession. He constantly reminds teachers and administrators about being caring and compassionate. It is with this in mind that he pursues his goal of assuring that children receive quality education in a nurturing environment. To maintain his link to his culture, he visits his homeland every year, spending time in a village on a remote island

www.ingramcontent.com/pod-product-compliance
Lightning Source LLC
Chambersburg PA
CBHW030257290526
45785CB00001B/126